Becoming a Video Game Artist

From Portfolio Design to Landing the Job

Becoming a Video Game Artist
From Portfolio Design to Landing the Job

John Pearl

CRC Press
Taylor & Francis Group
Boca Raton London New York

CRC Press is an imprint of the
Taylor & Francis Group, an **informa** business

AN A K PETERS BOOK

CRC Press
Taylor & Francis Group
6000 Broken Sound Parkway NW, Suite 300
Boca Raton, FL 33487-2742

© 2017 by Taylor & Francis Group, LLC
CRC Press is an imprint of Taylor & Francis Group, an Informa business

No claim to original U.S. Government works

Printed on acid-free paper
Version Date: 20160622

International Standard Book Number-13: 978-1-138-82493-5 (Paperback)

Library of Congress Cataloging-in-Publication Data

Names: Pearl, John, author.
Title: Becoming a video game artist : from portfolio design to landing the
job / John Pearl.
Description: Boca Raton : Taylor & Francis, a CRC title, part of the Taylor &
Francis imprint, a member of the Taylor & Francis Group, the academic
division of T&F Informa, plc, [2017]
Identifiers: LCCN 2016024612 | ISBN 9781138824935 (alk. paper)
Subjects: LCSH: Computer art--Vocational guidance. | Art portfolios. | Video
games industry--Vocational guidance.
Classification: LCC N7433.8 .P42 2017 | DDC 776--dc23
LC record available at https://lccn.loc.gov/2016024612

Visit the Taylor & Francis Web site at
http://www.taylorandfrancis.com

and the CRC Press Web site at
http://www.crcpress.com

Printed and bound in the United States of America by Sheridan

For Leah and Drake

Contents

7 Introduction to Being Technical Artist 63

Preface

There are more game companies than ever before, but there are also more individuals vying for game jobs than ever. An individual looking to break into the industry needs to set him/herself apart in any way they can from their competition. I've worked in the game industry for 17 years as of writing this book. In that time I've worked on more than a dozen games, held many different titles, and had the opportunity to review what feels like several thousand portfolios. After reviewing that many portfolios, you begin to see the same issues with content and presentation over and over again. With so many game schools, and online resources offering training for a career in games, it seems like these issues wouldn't be so prevalent. I wondered how I could still see the same mistakes in portfolios today that I made when I started out more than a decade and a half ago.

After looking around, I found that there wasn't a lot of resources about preparing a great portfolio and there were even less about the responsibilities of the actual positions within the video game field. How can people prepare a relevant portfolio if they don't understand the responsibilities of the job they're applying for? These are the things that drove me to write this book.

I knew I couldn't write this book alone or, if I did, it might come across as a single voice. While I've had the opportunity to work in many different art positions, I'm not an expert in all of them. I wanted this book to be as well rounded and as informative as possible. To accomplish this, I contacted some of the most seasoned talent across lots of different jobs that I've met during my career and some people I've never met in person to ask them to contribute to this project. Their answers and advice were better than I could've hoped for. This book is really a testament of the community within the games industry of people who want to see others succeed.

Acknowledgments

I would like to thank all the amazing people who contributed to this book. Without their perspectives and insight, this book wouldn't have been possible. Their personal experiences and advice are invaluable. I would also like to thank Reinhard Pollice of Nordic Games and David Adams of Gunfire Games for allowing me to use images from their games in this book. Additionally, I'd also like to thank Christopher J. Anderson, Ryan Gitter, and Melissa Smith for allowing me to use their personal work throughout this book.

For encouragement, support, and love, I thank my wonderful wife, Leah Pearl, and our son, Drake Sagan Pearl. Without their support, this book wouldn't have been a reality.

Author

John Pearl, Design Director/Principal Artist, Gunfire Games. Over the past 17 years, John has worked in the role of character artist, environment artist, lead environment artist, principal artist, environmental art director, character art director, and technical art director. While in those positions, he's worked a number of different styles and genres of games. The most notable to date was the *Darksiders Franchise* including the recent *Darksiders II: Deathinitive Edition.* He is one of the founders of Gunfire Games where they recently shipped Chronos for the Oculus Rift.

Contributors

Christopher J. Anderson, Senior Concept Artist, BioWare. Christopher J. Anderson has worked as a concept artist in the game industry for 14 years. He has worked for a number of different high-profile companies, including Mythic Entertainment, NCSoft, Tencent, Turbine, and BioWare Austin. During that time, he has worked as a senior and a lead on numerous projects that varied greatly in both style and scope. (http://chrisjandersonlatest.blogspot.com/)

Jay Bakke, Senior Visual Effects Artist, Bungie, Inc. In his 9 years of working experience in the video game industry, Jay Bakke has worked on several titles, including *Destiny, God of War: Ascension, Dungeon Siege 3*, and *Neverwinter Nights 2*. Jay is currently working at Bungie as a senior visual effects artist. Although most of his career has revolved around visual effects, his thirst to tackle complex tasks has led him to wear several other hats including animation, rigging, and tech art lighting. Prior to game development, Jay got his Bachelors in Animation at the Art Institute of Minneapolis. He then spent 3 years working as a 3d animator in the medical animation field, focused primarily on musculoskeletal work for the spinal surgery industry. Outside of game development, Jay enjoys cycling, hiking, and rebuilding classic cars.

Ben Cloward, CG Supervisor, BioWare Austin. Ben Cloward has been an animator and technical artist in the video game industry for 17 years. He started his career as an animator and worked for 8 years, breathing life into Robotech Mecha, monkeys (Curious George), and other fun characters. On the other side, Ben learned scripting and shader programing, and then made the transition to the tech art role. Ben is now focused on graphics and shaders as well as performance optimization. He lives with his wife and five kids in Austin, Texas. (http://www.bencloward.com/)

Cory Edwards, Senior World Artist, Bethesda Game Studios. After graduating from Savannah College of Art and Design, Cory Edwards landed a job at Terminal Reality working on *BloodRayne 2* and then on *AeonFlux*. After his time there, he moved onto Paradigm Entertainment where he worked on *Stuntman 2*. Once finished on *Stuntman 2*, he moved onto Bethesda Game Studios where he works currently. While there he had the chance to work on big games like *Fallout 3* and *4* as well as *The Elder Scrolls V: Skyrim* and it's post launch content as well.

Ryan Gitter, Senior Concept Artist, Bungie. Ryan Gitter is a concept artist working in the game industry. Originally from Michigan, Ryan moved to Austin, Texas, in 2009 to begin a career in the video games. Since then he has worked on titles from *Starhawk* to *Call of Duty: Ghosts, Halo 4, Halo MCC*, and several others. He has recently moved on to work at Bungie. (http://www.gitterart.com/, https://www.patreon.com/user?u=478476)

Jeff Hanna, Principal Technical Artist, Volition. A 21-year veteran of the video game industry, Jeff Hanna has worked on many notable franchises, such as *Saints Row, Red Faction, Planetside*, and *Dark Age of Camelot*. He currently works at Volition, helping to create and refine their game-creation tools and pipelines. He is also involved with Purdue University's Computer Graphics department, where he helps define the curriculum for the school and lecture to students in their senior-level capstone class. Jeff has been a member of the GDC Advisory Board for 7 years. He was awarded an Autodesk 3ds Max Master award in 2007 and was named an Outstanding Alum of Purdue University in 2012.

Patrick Ingoldsby, Art Director/ Ubisoft Toronto. Patrick Ingoldsby entered the games industry in 1998 when 3d graphics gained a foothold in both animation and games production. Feeling very optimistic about the future of 3d graphics and what advancing visual technology could provide for games, he accepted a 3d artist role at Silicon Knights.

Being a lifelong artist and fan of games, cinema, and graphic novels, Patrick found the perfect industry that allowed him to flourish artistically and work with other creative people. He never looked back.

For most of his career, Patrick contributed 3d environment art and led various production art teams on many AAA titles. His contributions include modeling, texturing, level art, level design, and principal lighting on many releases including *Eternal Darkness, Metal Gear Solid—The Twin Snakes, Too Human, Darksiders, Splinter Cell Blacklist*, and *Assassin's Creed Unity*.

In 2010, Ubisoft Toronto opened its doors and Patrick has been busy providing art direction for many visual teams on Ubisoft premium brands.

Brian "Bobo" Jones, Principal Artist/Co-Founder OMNOM! Workshop. Brian Jones (also known as BoBo the seal) is a principal artist and co-founder at OMNOM! workshop. Brian started his career in the industry in 2000 and has worked at seven studios and has contributed to over game related 60 projects. Most notably, *Darksiders II, League of Legends, Diablo III, Age of Empires III*, and *Titan Quest*. (http://www.omnomworkshop.com/)

Tohan Kim, Senior Character Artist, Gunfire Games. Tohan has worked as a character artist in games for more than 16 years. He started out at Bethesda Softworks where he worked on *Elder Scrolls III: Morrowind* doing concept art, modeling, texturing, and animation. After that he moved onto Mythic as a character artist, then later as a senior character artist where he worked on *Dark Age of Camelot, Warhammer Age of Reckoning*, and *Dragon Age II*. He then joined Vigil Games where he worked on *Darksiders II*. After Vigil, he went onto Crytek USA where he worked on *Hunt: Horrors of the Gilded Age*. He currently works as a senior character artist at Gunfire Games. (https://www.artstation.com/artist/tohankim)

Leisel Madureira, Animator, Gunfire Games. Leisel Madureira grew up in Austin, Texas, and has been a lifelong animation fan. She went to the Art Institute of Dallas to study 2d and 3d animation. She first started her career at Vigil Games as an intern before becoming a full-time animator working on *Darksiders* and *Darksiders II*. She was with Vigil for almost 6 years before the closing of THQ. She now works as an animator at Gunfire Games.

Steve Madureira, Lead Animator, Airship Syndicate. Steve Madureira has been working in the industry as an animator for 10 years. He began his career with Vigil Games as an animation intern when the company was in its inception, being the 7th employee. He stayed with Vigil Games until it was shut down in late January 2013. While being there, he eventually became a senior animator and worked on *Darksiders I* and *Darksiders II*.

After the closure of Vigil Games, Steve was part of the team that formed Crytek USA. While there, he did additional animations on *Ryse* and worked on *Hunt*. Steve left Crytek and started a new company, Airship Syndicate, with two of the founders of Vigil Games.

Lindsey McQueeny, Lead Recruiter, Crystal Dynamics. Lindsey McQueeny is a compulsive nostalgic JRPG gamer who has clocked at least 1000 hours on just the Final Fantasy series alone, and has been the infamous survivor/adventurer Lara Croft for Halloween at least twice, thus basically paving the yellow brick path to her dream job as lead recruiter for Crystal Dynamics Inc., subsidiary of Square-Enix. With both great pride and great humility, she's been enthusiastically hiring the most remarkable, awe-inspiring talent this industry has to offer for going on 9 years.

She is a regular presenter/speaker regarding best practices for networking, portfolio creation, and the application/interviewing process for entry-level positions in the game development industry and is passionate about mentoring the game development industry leaders of the future on how to get noticed for all the right reasons rather than all the wrong ones.

Chris Mead, Animation Director, Gunfire Games. Shortly after graduating from the University of Texas with a Bachelor of Fine Arts degree in 1995, Chris Mead got his first job in games with Human Code. This studio made interactive CD-ROM games for clients such as Discovery Channel, Hasbro, and Time-Life Books. Chris started his career as a Photoshop illustrator. He mostly painted background images in Photoshop for 2D, sprite-based games. He soon transitioned to animating the 2d sprites as well as doing some interface design. During this time, Chris took the initiative to learn 3d modeling and animation. In 1999, Chris convinced studio management that he could model and animate all the characters for a project they were bidding on for Mattel. With a successful demonstration of 3d animation, he helped the studio land the contract for *Barbie Riding Club*. When the game was released a year later, it was the top-selling game that holiday season. Chris's career has been focused on 3d animation ever since.

Mike Nicholson, Senior UI Designer, Blizzard Entertainment. Mike Nicholson has been in the gaming industry since 1994 where he started as a pixel artist. Over the years, he has dabbled in art and design and eventually gravitated to user interface. He is one of those lucky folks whose job also happens to be his favorite hobby. He understands if you hate him for that. Aside from games, he enjoys walks on the beach, a good margarita, and writing about himself in the third person. (http://mikenart.wix.com/portfolio)

Adam Pitts, Senior Character Artist, Arkane Studios. Adam Pitts has been in the games industry for more than 11 years and has worked as an art generalist on a range of projects. Shipped titles include—*Prince of Persia: Warrior Within, StarWars: Empire at War, Star Wars: Forces of Corruption, Universe at War: Earth Assault, DC Universe Online*, and *Darksiders II*. He currently works at Arkane Studios focusing primarily on character art.

Ryan Rosanky, Lead Visual Effects Artist (*Dragon Age Inquisition*) BioWare, Edmonton. Ryan Rosanky is a lead visual effects artist at BioWare Edmonton who has worked in the game industry for more than 11 years. He has had the privilege to work on some pretty amazing titles, such as *Mass Effect, Darksiders*, and just recently led the Visual Effects team on *Dragon Age Inquisition*.

Keith Self-Ballard, Principal Artist, Deep Silver Volition. Keith is a veteran world builder in the games industry. His contributions include entries in the Myst and Everquest franchises. During his 7-year term with THQ|Volition Inc., Keith functioned as a lead environment artist, art department manager, and eventually studio art director during the development of *Red Faction Guerrilla* and *Saints Row: The Third*. He spent 2 years managing world development at

Blizzard Entertainment on the studio's "Next-Gen MMO" before transitioning to art training manager for the studio. Keith is currently employed as a principal artist at Deep Silver Volition where he functions as the project's environment art director. (Art & Leadership Blog; hyphenatedkeith.blogspot.com)

Melissa Smith, Environment Artist, Sony Santa Monica. Melissa Smith is an environment artist and has been developing games since 2008. She is currently at Sony Santa Monica. Recently, she has worked on *Sunset Overdrive*. She graduated from The University of Texas at Dallas and got her big break in games at Vigil Games working on *Darksiders*. Her enthusiasm for colorful, energetic, and vivid art has led her to work on many diverse titles at many studios. Through her studio involvement, she has experienced the excitement of working for startup studios and the heartbreak of veteran studio closures. Her dedication is an example of the hard work and passion required to thrive in the collaborative world of game development. (cargocollective.com/melmelsmith)

Samuel Tung, Developer Relations Engineer—Technical Art, Amazon. Samuel has worked as technical artist in games for more than 11 years. He attended Vancouver Film School and was then chosen to travel to France as part of the Supinfocom Graduate Exchange Program. After graduating, he went on to work at Activision where he was part of the Central Technology group where he worked on a large number of well-known franchises including *Call of Duty, Transformers*, and *Tony Hawk*. After leaving Activision, he joined THQ's XDG (External Development Group) and worked as a senior tech artist and then as a technical art manager on some of THQ's biggest franchises: *Saint's Row, Homefront, Warhammer 40k, Metro*, and *Darksiders*. He then joined the team at Turtle Rock Studios to work on *Evolve* as the lead technical artist and outsourcing manager. He currently works for Amazon in the role of developer relations engineer—Technical Art for Core Game Technology group.

Laura Zimmermann, Lead Environment Artist, Certain Affinity. Growing up in rural Wisconsin, and graduating from a school with one of the lowest funded art programs in the state, Laura had extremely high aspirations when she decided to attend the Ringling College of Art and Design in 2000. She always had a desire to do drawing and painting, and went to college with the goal of graduating in their illustration department, but with no real plan with what to do with it afterward—only that she wanted to continue doing art professionally. Luckily, she discovered that her talents were both needed and desired in the video games industry. EA-Tiburon in Orlando, Florida hired her right out of school to work on numerous projects, including *Nascar Racing, Madden Football*, and *Superman Returns*. While she started out doing purely texture work, her colleagues took the time and effort to nurture her aspirations to become a more well-rounded artist, and they taught her skills in 3d. With their help and urging, she was able to secure a full environment artist position at EA-Tiburon and continue working on her 3d skills in a professional setting. In 2006, Laura was offered the chance to move to Irrational Games in Boston, Massachusetts, to work on a highly anticipated project called *Bioshock*. She stayed for another 7 years, not only to work on *Bioshock*, but also *Bioshock Infinite*, as well as some side projects. At Irrational Games, Laura was not only able to work on projects that utilized and challenged all of her skills, but also able to work on games that she herself would want to play. With the unfortunate closing of Irrational Games in early 2014, she looked to Austin, Texas, in hopes that she could secure a position closer to family in the area. Fortunately, Certain Affinity hired her as their newest senior environment artist, and she has been living happily in Texas since May 2014, working on projects such as *Halo: The Master Chief Collection*, as well as other unannounced projects. When not doing art, Laura enjoys reading, writing, practicing martial arts, and trying to wrangle a small herd of cats around her apartment.

1

Introduction

How I Got into Games

When I speak to anyone who wants to get into game development, I'm not surprised that frequently their first question is: "How did you get into games?" The answer to the question is always interesting and everyone's "origin story" is quite different.

When I was in college, there were no game development courses or curriculums available. At the time, the PlayStation 1 and Nintendo 64 were the current generation of gaming hardware and 3d had taken center stage in games. I knew that I wanted to work on games, but I didn't really understand how to accomplish this. I enrolled in an art college that offered something called "Time-Based Media Studies" because it was the only major that involved computer animation. In addition to computer animation, the major also involved traditional animation, storyboarding, and film and video production. This major was part of the curriculum that was built up on a strong foundation of traditional art that included figure drawing, painting, color theory, and 2d and 3d designs. The idea of 3d computer animation wasn't new or novel at the time; it had been used for years in movies and games. However, schools didn't really have a solid plan for properly training people to prepare for a job in computer animation, let alone what was needed to make an impressive portfolio to get you noticed.

The emphasis at my school on traditional art fundamentals meant that I went 2 years before getting into my major. Having this traditional art background has proven invaluable to me over the years I've worked in the industry; however, it wasn't apparent it would be at the time. During my junior year, I got into my major and spent every waking moment working in 3d, making characters, environments, and eventually animating them. I didn't really know what positions were out there, what was expected of entry-level artists or even what to put in my portfolio. My senior portfolio class taught that it was good to "cover all the bases," so my portfolio was a mixture of character work, environment art, an animated short, video work, and traditional animation. The problem with this was I ended up showing that I could do a lot of different things; however, without a specific focus, my energy was split amongst different disciplines. The end result was that none of it stood out because I hadn't had the proper time or direction to refine any one part of it.

I struggled to find work after graduating and wasn't sure why, since I hit all the checkboxes on what I had thought was a "complete" portfolio. Even after not garnering any interest from my portfolio, I continued to spread my time equally amongst the different disciplines, still not understanding what I was "missing." What I was missing was focus and refinement. I hadn't picked a specific craft and gave it my all. I began to gravitate toward environments and character work, abandoning 2d and 3d animations and video work. After doing that I was able to finally land an interview and get my foot in the door; however, it still didn't get me the job. A friend and classmate of mine, Christopher J. Anderson, got a job as a Concept Artist with DreamForge Intertainment and continued to put in a good word for me to the art director. While he did this, I would touch base with the art director to follow up every couple weeks. Eventually, more positions opened up and due to my persistence they gave me an art test. At the time, art tests weren't as common as they are today, but I was happy to get the opportunity to prove myself. I turned it around in a day and heard back from them with an offer almost immediately.

I worked at DreamForge Intertainment for about a year. I started as a character artist, and after finishing the bulk of the planned character work, I moved onto environments. During this time, they lost their publisher and had a large layoff. Almost to the day, a year after I was hired, they closed down. This is not unusual, and, as you'll see and probably heard, it's quite common in games. Projects get canceled, publishers close, and any of number of things can occur outside of normal development that will directly affect you and the project you are working on. How and what occurs at a company when this happens is directly related to how the company is operated and how well they plan their finances. That isn't to say that a company with impeccable financial planning won't close; it's just less likely if they have backup plans.

After the closure of DreamForge, I found myself in a familiar position. I again needed to prepare a portfolio; this time I was somewhat better equipped to produce a game-relevant portfolio as I had a year of experience under my belt. I took a few months to work on my portfolio as I didn't feel that the content I had created the previous year was well rounded enough to get a job. It played a major role in the content of my portfolio; however, it was a specific genre and style and I wanted to include a larger variety of content to show my expanded skillset. After completing my new portfolio, I submitted it to several companies that I was interested in. I heard back almost immediately from a company called Paradigm Entertainment. Even after spending a few months generating content specifically for my portfolio, they wanted me to perform an art test. Like the previous time, I completed the art to the best of my ability and heard back almost immediately.

I worked at Paradigm for about 5 years and eventually left for California to a company called Stormfront Studios. I spent a few years there before moving on. If these company names don't sound familiar, there's a reason behind it: they're all closed. This is unfortunately, a pretty good representation of how volatile the game industry can be. All of them had pretty big games at one point or another, but that doesn't matter. From Stormfront, I moved on to Vigil Games where I helped create the Darksiders Franchise. After *Darksiders II* and our canceled massively multiplayer online (MMO) project we started a new project, but were shut down after THQ went bankrupt. A smaller group of us were hired on to start up Crytek USA. After a year there and financial troubles, they too closed. This actually occurred while I was writing this very book! After Crytek USA closed, the leadership team from Crytek USA, which was also a good portion of the leadership team from Vigil Games, got together and decided to start a new independent company, Gunfire Games. In the short time we've been open we've been able to ship several games including *Darksiders II: Deathinitive Edition* and *Chronos* for the Oculus Rift.

Why Write This Book?

During the last 16 years, I've worked as a character artist, environment artist, lead environment artist, principal artist, environmental art director, character art director, and technical art director. While in those positions, I've worked closely with artists in other disciplines such as concept art, user interface, visual effects, and animation. I've also reviewed hundreds upon hundreds of portfolios for various art positions and run several successful internship programs at Vigil Games.

As I mentioned, when I first got into games, there wasn't a lot of resources or information about the different types of art-related game jobs available. Today with forums and game-career sites, there are more resources available; however, I still see the same mistakes and problems with portfolio submissions that I was doing over a decade and a half ago. I feel like there aren't enough collected resources so I've written this book that I would've wanted when I first started looking for a job in game development. Filled with detailed descriptions on the types of jobs, their responsibilities, and required skillsets as well as interviews with working professionals about their experiences and career advice, I realize this book can't be in everyone's hands but my hope is that anyone who does read it will feel a lot more informed when putting together a portfolio and applying for their dream job.

"Some Companies"

One thing you may find reference to a lot in this book is "some companies." I say that as a caveat because every company is different. These differences could be slight, or they could be significant. This goes for hiring practices, for benefits, for how they schedule a game to how they provide feedback. Some companies are quite rigid and have very strict processes in place that their organization follows, while others are a lot more relaxed. The reason for this is that companies can form in many different ways and often that can inform how they are run. If a large company opens up a new studio, they will often put key people in leadership roles to ensure that a certain structure and culture are in place. A studio that is formed by a small group of individuals will likely develop its culture more organically and play to the strengths of those individuals and create their rules accordingly.

It's important to understand this because it will help you to determine if the company is a good fit for you. It's worth mentioning that there is no catch-all advice that covers every game studio. A studio head with a production background will often run a studio very differently than the one with a programming background, for example. It's hard to know exactly how a company is run until you're working there and even then it may not be entirely obvious from the start. It's not a bad idea to do research on a company before applying as it may give you some insight into the studio culture and how successful you can be there.

Stability

I like to warn anyone who is looking to start their career in games that they need to be realistic not only about their expectations of the work but also about the lack of stability in game jobs. Game companies come and go, games get canceled, games ship, and teams still get hit with layoffs. It's the reality of a "hits-driven" industry. Larger games cost more and more to make, and with that they need to sell more copies in order to be considered successes. For a bit of perspective, I'm at my 6th company in 16 years. The first five companies I worked for are all closed. Some closed while I was there, some closed shortly after I left. The point is: You should always be prepared for situations like this to occur. I'm not a financial advisor, but it's smart to hold some of your paycheck back as a rainy day fund just "in case" you find yourself out of work.

Attention to Detail Exercises

Throughout this book, you will find "attention to detail" exercises that take real-world objects, concepts, or other images, and examine some of the smaller details that often are overlooked when artists craft something similar in 3d or 2d design. It is easy to focus on particular details and miss some details that help sell the believability of an object, character or location. An eye for detail is an attribute every artist should have; however, it often doesn't come naturally. It is, however, a skill that can be focused and refined over time. The goal of these brief exercises is to get you as a reader to start refining those skills and thinking about the subtle details that you can add to your work to make them stand out.

2

General Concepts and Skills

How Do You Get into Games?

If you're reading this book, you've probably said at one point, "I want to work on games," "I want to make art for games," or even "I know exactly what I want to do, I just don't know how to get there." The question I often asked myself before becoming a professional game developer was: "How can I craft a portfolio for a job when I don't fully understand what the responsibilities of the positions are?"

In the first portion of this book, we'll delve into different art positions and the responsibilities that go with them. The most common art-related game development positions we'll look at are as follows: animator, environment artist, concept artist, character artist, technical artist, visual effects artist, and UI artist. In each chapter related to a specific discipline, I've listed out some key skills found on many high-profile company job listings for the specific positions. We'll then look at preparing portfolio content for those positions as it's helpful to understand expectations when putting together your collected work. However, before getting into specific position details and setting up a portfolio, we'll look at some general skills and responsibilities required for any game art position. Additionally, we'll also hear from some of this book's contributors about their thoughts on the general skills every game developer should possess.

Excellent Communication Skills

Excellent communication skills aren't just the ability to speak well, which is necessary, but the ability to listen, comprehend, and retain information is just as important, if not more. Giving another person your full attention in a conversation means that you will likely retain more of the information and be able to ask meaningful follow-up questions. Staying relevant in game development means that you are always learning, and the best place to learn new things is from your peers. Game development is a group effort, and it takes people from a variety of disciplines to make an idea into a reality. Always take advantage of the knowledge that is around you and don't be afraid to ask questions when you don't know something or speak up when you do know something.

Excellent communication skills also include the ability to deliver your message clearly with purpose and intent. Great communication is a two-way street, and it means that you understand and you are understood. Understanding your "audience" and tailoring your message to that audience means that the message will be better received. Learning to appreciate other's points of view and their goals can help you work to align your goals to achieve something bigger than you can on your own. Good communication is not limited to in-person conversations; like most communication in the world, a lot of it is handled through email and instant message (IM). Text is devoid of emotional context so it's imperative to avoid words that can be viewed as aggressive or confrontational. Learning how to craft an email that informs quickly yet to the point while not coming across as curt or informal can be a challenging task.

Now that we've established what good communication skills entail, why are they so important in game development? Game development has a lot of moving parts and interdependencies at all times. Different people are often working concurrently on different parts of a bigger task. It's important that those people are in sync with each other and updated as small and large changes can and do often occur. An example would be a creature designer (CD) provides a write-up for a large blue monster with six arms. This write-up is passed onto the concept art team and the concept artist begins drawing thumbnail sketches of the creature. Working with the art director (AD), they find the creature is more visually compelling if it's orange with four arms. This is approved and passed onto the character artist to create the model. Meanwhile, the CD may be working with the animation team planning out attacks and movement based on six arms, not four, and they may feel that it would be cool to add a fire tail as well. At the same time, the visual effects artist may begin working on effects for a blue creature not an orange one and assuming that there will be six arms and knows nothing of the fire tail. This could go on and on, where different departments are getting further and further away from each other by working toward different end goals.

In situations like this, it's assumed that these things will just be caught by someone else, or that it's someone else's job to stay up to minute with changes as they occur and keep people informed. While that is the responsibility of producers and associate producers on a project, the reality is that they can't be everywhere at all times, and what I described can occur in the course of a single day and is based on a few seemingly negligible changes. This can, however, result in days of wasted work for multiple people and departments. Anyone in that chain should feel comfortable to update other departments about changes, as well as seek out any pertinent updates on their tasks.

Another reason communication skills are significant is that they allow you to contribute even more to the game and eventually may help lead to a promotion. The ability to articulate your ideas and give thoughtful, insightful feedback is an essential skill in developing your career. The ability to speak to your peers in a respective and productive way about ideas for the game is an important process in your growth as a developer. Leads and directors will appreciate you taking the time to give thoughtful feedback, but importantly your ability to let go of your ideas if they are not used. Often as a young game developer, you are ready to set the world on fire with your passion and ideas. While it's important to maintain this level of passion throughout your career, it's also imperative to learn that there are reasons that not all ideas can be used some of which being feasibility, schedule, or simply not fitting with the larger game vision. Having the maturity to let ideas go and move on is part of the process of growing as a game developer.

Interview

What General Skills Do You Feel Are Important for Any Game Developer?

Leisel Madureira: Communication, and the ability to work well with others. You might not be the most talented or skilled developer on the team, but if you're easy to work with and people like working with you, that will carry you a long way. Crunch is common and developers want to work with others they won't hate by the end of a project. That and a good reputation will likely follow you the next time you find yourself applying for another job. Chances are they might have heard about you already from someone you use to work with and now works at the studio you're now applying to. A bad reputation can cost you a job no matter how talented you are.

Cory Edwards: Communication. Basic social skills. Being friendly.

Keith Self-Ballard: Solid communication skills are a must. Making games requires a range of talents and the ability to collaborate with a variety of people and opinions is required (unless you're a solo independent developer). It's vital that you are able to present your ideas, your work, and your goals. Moreover, it's important to learn how to listen to and understand the ideas, the work, and the goals of others.

Brian "Bobo" Jones: Communication and organization. Remember you are a step in a production line. You need to know what the other members of the team need from you to make the game as a whole not just your individual asset.

Collaboration

Building upon the foundation of solid communication is another frequent requirement in job postings: collaboration. Very few games are made by one person; most games require a team of skilled individuals to come together to create the final product. I've always felt in the game industry that you have the potential, more than in most of industries, to have some of the most vastly different types of personalities and skill sets working together toward a common goal. This isn't just working with artists who have different opinions on art, but with people who have completely different ways of thinking and completely different goals in their work. The differences, for example, in both personalities and methodologies between artists and programmers can be huge. Introduce sound engineers, game designers, and producers into that mix and you have a lot of people who have diverse priorities in regard to the final game. Programmers may focus on functionality and stability, where designers may be focused on game flow and fun, while sound designers are focused on audio cues and the quality of the sound experience.

The variety of personalities and the need for those contributions from the individuals is why collaboration is such an important skill. No one on a game team works in a vacuum. Everyone's work affects the other members of the team, both directly and indirectly. Environment artists must work closely with level designers to craft the game world, character artists work closely with animators, and animators, in turn, work closely with game designers; concept artists and tech artists work with everyone but in very different capacities (see Figure 2.1). This goes beyond having good "people skills." It comes down to understanding

Figure 2.1

A piece of concept work and its final asset that serves as an example of collaboration between a concept artist and a character artist. Concept by Avery Coleman and character by Tohan Kim. (Used with the permission of Nordic Games.)

2. General Concepts and Skills

what the goals of the other team members are and being able to make good compromises for the betterment of the game as a whole even if it means making sacrifices to your personal work.

Interview

What General Skills Do You Feel Are Important for Any Game Developer?

Jay Bakke: Be a good teammate, stay humble, and be open to other people's opinions. It is also good to stay up to date with developments in big budget games as well as the unique ideas coming out of indie game circuit.

Ryan Rosanky: Talk to your coworkers. Find out as much as you can about the project and what is going on outside the company in other studios. Keep current on latest plug-ins and new bells and whistles that can help make your game better.

Adam Pitts: Be humble. No one wants to work with someone who has an ego problem. It's a small industry and everyone knows someone at another studio. If you're a pain to work with, your opportunities will shrink. Also, be a problem solver. We regularly face technical limitations that require creative work around. Be ready to think outside of the box.

Mike Nicholson: A sense of humor, a thick skin, and the ability to accept change. Games are constantly evolving from both a technological and market standpoint. Be ready to adapt, be as good natured as you can be, and be an asset to anyone's team.

Prototyping

During the course of a game's production, many artists will be required to "prototype" something. This could be a new way to concept characters, a new weapon, a new character type, a new animation technique, or even a new pipeline. This is often front loaded into the preproduction period of a game, but will still occur with some frequency over the course of a project. Prototyping is a generic term in games used to describe a new attempt, new implementation, or a new spin on something for the game. It's often "new" in regard to the engine, game, or team, but not necessarily new to the game industry as a whole. Game teams often have to find their own way of doing things because what worked for one team may not work for another due to available resources, team composition, or available tools. One way to think of prototyping in games is like a hypothesis in science where a proposed idea must be tested to see if it is feasible and if it will work.

For environment artists, this can mean attempting a new system that involves modular set pieces, a new level layout, or even a new art style for the game. For animators, it could mean a new approach to integrating motion capture data, a new skeletal rig system, or an introduction of automation or batching into the pipeline. For character artists, it could mean trying out a new weapon type, character style experiments, or even introducing a new program into the pipeline for asset creation. For tech artists, it could mean supporting any of the above or creating a new process or pipeline entirely.

A production artist should never see any of their work as sacred, this is even more important when doing prototype work. Things change during the course of a game's development, work may need to be redone or completely thrown away. It's important to be fluid and go with the flow because if you don't accept that this is a part of game development early on in your career, it can lead to a lot of frustration. Prototypes are often meant to be loose and rough because the goal is often speed and method discovery not polish. Once the prototype has been proven to be successful, it will usually be integrated into the game or pipeline. Even if the prototyping was not successful, there was still knowledge to be gained from the endeavor.

Problem Solving

This really is a core skill for any game developer; however, the variety and breadth of issues and technical challenges an artist faces during the course of a game's development can be quite varied. This can range from defective tools, broken pipelines, integration problems to even asset issues. Sometimes as an artist you can work through it and solve the problems on your own, whether they are visual or technical. Other times it's not apparent what the problem is, but it can be obvious that there is one, and it is a matter of working backward from the problem to discover the cause of the issue.

In some cases, you may need support from technical artists or even the programming team. This is where good communication comes into play once again. Being able to articulate the problem you are experiencing with as much technically relevant data possible will determine how fast you can get to a solution. The most crucial skill that determines how fast your problem gets solved is your ability to replicate and document the process up to the broken step. This process can provide a valuable insight to help solve the problem. This information can then be used by you or someone else to come up with a solution. Providing simple, repeatable test cases can mean the difference between hours or days for getting a problem fixed. This process is very similar to how quality assurance testers find and document bugs in a game.

The other side of problem solving for an artist comes in the form of visual problem solving. This usually involves solving artistic challenges like consistency of a visual style, readability, color palettes, and shape design. Every animation, concept, or 3d model will have a degree of problem solving that needs to go in into it. The bigger task of visual problem solving occurs when something has not been attempted before in the game or there is not an approved visual style or process in place. This can overlap with the ideas mentioned previously in regard to prototyping; however, it doesn't necessarily have to. This could take the form of a character artist receiving a rough or partial concept for an asset and then needing to extrapolate the rest of the character from it. This may take the form of an animator finding a process to quickly but believably transition between two dissimilar animations to avoid making the character control awkwardly. Every art discipline has its own set of visual problems it needs to solve. This is important because companies are looking for people who can step up and solve these problems without a lot of hand-holding or oversight.

Lastly, problem solving can take the form of working within technical artistic limitations. This type of problem solving comes in many forms during the course of development for the different artists on the team. Technical artists focus on this most of the time; however, every artist deals with it in some capacity or another. Concept artists may be given restrictions on the design of a character. For example, a character may need to adhere to a specific visual style and technical parameters that may at first feel diametrically opposed. It is up to the concept artist to find a compromise that doesn't end up sacrificing too much of either direction. Character artists may have to deal with things like memory constraints while making sure that their characters have enough fidelity both in texture and polycount. Environment artists may have to craft a level with lofty visual goals with very few resources to do so. This is where creativity on a technical problem-solving standpoint comes into play. Every artist should look to learn as much as they can each time they encounter these technical hurdles as they will be a better artist for it.

Attention to Detail

In the first Attention to Detail exercise, we're going to look at an old car (Figure 2.2). The key thing to take away from this exercise is that whether you're concepting, modeling or texturing; rust often has a very predictable distribution on surfaces.

Figure 2.2

This is an old car with lots of interesting character that would translate well into a game asset. A–D focuses on some of the details that help to build a convincing asset. (Copyright iStock.com/Eduardo Luzzatti Buyé. With permission.)

A. First thing to notice is the chrome bumper is covered in rust. You can tell that the rust was caused by water as you can see the streaks in the form of rust the water caused down the front of the bumper.

B. Most rust on metal occurs where the metal and another surface touch and water is allowed to sit. This is most likely what caused the rust to start around the front grill.

C. If this were a 3d model, this would be an excellent use of asymmetry. Notice that the protective chrome frame is missing from around the light on this side of the car.

D. The other thing that can cause the degradation of metal, particularly on cars, is oil from human hands and any sort of repetitive wear that degrades the protectant coat on the paint. In this case, the area around the door handles is rusted, while the rest of the door is comparatively clean. This is due to the shear amount of hands and objects coming in contact with the handle so many times a day.

Creativity

This skill is sometimes overlooked by people trying to get into games or when crafting their portfolio. "I do art, which is a creative skill; therefore, I am creative." Creativity isn't just a check box of a resume, but a way of thinking and solving problems. It is about approaching an idea or task with a unique or fresh perspective on it. It's also about bringing something new or meaningful to an existing idea. This comes into play in every discipline in game development. This is often because no problem is the same as previous ones and no solution fits all cases.

As a game artist, it's important to show your creativity in your portfolio. This not only means fresh takes and interesting twists and well-worn concepts in regard to your content, but also how you achieved your results. This may mean approaching something differently in the way the asset was created or how the final result was achieved. Some examples of this would be how the texture was created on a character, how shaders were used and applied in a scene, or how an effect was animated. There is a lot of room for new and creative approaches to old ideas. Don't be afraid to break out of the mold and attempt something different.

Organization

Organization is a key element in game development. This comes into play in almost every aspect of game development; from how you name your files to how you set up your layers in Photoshop to how you manage your schedule. Staying organized not only allows you to work efficiently, but it also helps your teammates. Rarely is a single person the first and last individual to work with a given file. For this reason, you need to learn how to keep your files clean and organized, as well as how to name and store them in an efficient manner. On a team, when it comes to storing your work, this usually means uploading them onto a server by way of source control software like Perforce. Once on the job, it will be important to learn the workflow and methods of the company in regard to how the files are named and stored.

Game development is all about team work and collaboration, so this means that others will depend on the work you do to be handed off to them in a clean and usable state. For some people, this comes naturally, and for others this is a very hard thing to learn as it may be counter to how they work. In either situation, you want your files to be clean and easily navigated for yourself and others. It's important to learn that art for a game is never really done until the game is shipped. For this reason, artists will often need to go back to their previous files or to other people's files and make updates. The reason for this can vary greatly, but some examples might be new shaders were created and older assets needed to be updated. Another reason might be a new type of game play has been added into the game, and older files may need to be adjusted to account for this. The list of reasons can go on and on. The thing that is important is the file you work on is clean when it's submitted, because you never know when or who may need to revisit it.

Working under Deadlines

If you are going through school or have gone through school, you understand deadlines. However, game deadlines or milestones as they are referred to in games are often much harder than any school assignment. The reason for this is that there are so many more moving parts in a game's development than any school project or group project. Internally, at a studio, you may depend on other disciplines to provide you with the design or tools you need to finish what is assigned to you, whereas externally, if there is a publisher involved, there may be marketing demos or large direction shifts that affect the game at large and thusly affect a given milestone. Other external issues may include updates to crucial third party software the team is using.

What this comes down to is developing good time-management skills. External issues mentioned may derail your progress; however, as an individual, you need to manage your time well and be very adaptable to any changes that come. Good time management often comes with experience; however, that is not an excuse to not work on it right away. As a developer starting out, you won't have a lot of experience to build your time-management skills. However, there are things that you can do to help properly manage your time.

The first thing to learn is to not let tools get in your way. Most of the time you spend working on something should be spent working on it, not navigating around tools that are broken or that you are unfamiliar with. If you find a process that seems tedious or takes longer than expected ask your peers or look for alternatives online. It's always okay to ask questions, especially if they result in speeding up your workflow. Tools are always being written, programs are always getting newer versions, methods are always changing, and there may be faster options you are not aware of. There is no shame in not knowing the latest tool for everything in a given pipeline.

Another element of time management is being aware of distractions and ancillary activities. Some things can be distractions for people without them even realizing it. These can be things like continuous IM conversations, checking social networking sites, and even watching a video on the second monitor. While these may seem harmless and help your focus, this is not the case; in fact, it is quite opposite. All of these things require diverting attention from a priority task to something else, whether it's switching over to a different window to check status updates, respond to an IM, or clicking next on the streaming video service; they all have an impact on productivity and speed at finishing a task.

Interview

What General Skills Do You Feel Are Important for Any Game Developer?

Patrick Ingoldsby: Time management! Working out your objectives and tasks within project timelines.

Many teams have production managers that help with this, but as an artist you need to be organized enough to manage yourself to a certain capacity. It takes discipline to process the deliverables required within realistic time blocks. And artists need to keep those blocks in mind in order to focus accordingly. Production management is an "art" all unto itself.

Being resourceful is another. Knowing how to learn, how to effectively research and develop when it's needed. Knowing where to collect the best reference material and how to get it when finding it is a challenge.

Passion for Games

A prerequisite on a lot of job posting is "a passion for games." This seems obvious, of course, you love games; why else would you be applying? However, when you think about it, it's kind of a strange requirement to actually post. You wouldn't see a job opening at an insurance company that has a line "passionate about insurance" or "passionate about insuring people." If anything it would say something about a "passion for helping or working with people," but not directly about the work itself. The line about "passion for games" can be easily glossed over, but here's why it's there: Making games is HARD work, and it's a labor of love to see it through to the end. There can be points in development where the only thing that can keep you going is that passion. The passion for games doesn't mean that you just enjoy playing them; it's a passion for how games are made and how they work.

Even as an artist in games, technical insight is a key component to your success. This will come naturally in time if you want to understand how games really work. Ignoring that side of development can severely limit your long-term success and overall contribution to a game. This can also lead to burnout as a game artist. A keen understanding of game development and internal systems can go a long way as an artist and keeping you passionate about your work. It also allows you to be involved in important conversations and speak from a position of knowledge as opposed to just having work assigned to you.

Passion for games not only means that you enjoy game making, but it also means that you stay relevant with modern games, not all of them, of course, but at least staying aware of current trends in the game market. There's a language in every video game company spoken on a daily basis and it's that of referential video game content. Current and recent games are referenced frequently in conversations, and staying abreast of the latest gaming concepts and achievements is crucial to understanding these conversations. Being able to dissect and understand how and why other games implement their art and design is a crucial step in maturing as a game developer.

It can be easy to say that you're passionate about your work or games; however, it's something that needs to be shown through your work. If you're not passionate about a project you're working on for your portfolio, it will come through to the viewer. When someone is truly excited about what they are creating, it comes across in the little detail and the level of attention they put in an animation or a concept or a character. Your goal should be to excite the people with your work, and they should be able to see the excitement you've put into it.

Interview

What General Skills Do You Feel Are Important for Any Game Developer?

Steve Madureira: I think playing games is important for any game developer. Understanding your craft is important to doing it better.

Laura Zimmermann: I do know a handful of artists within the game industry who don't play games, and I don't think it hampers their abilities at all. However, I think it is important for an artist (or any game developer) to be able to put themselves in the mindset of a player and to be able to see the game from their perspective. Knowing your audience is vital to understanding what needs to be conveyed on the screen, and why—either from a story perspective, or just from simply trying to properly sell the environment in which the game is set.

Tohan Kim: "Great companies don't hire skilled people and motivate them. They hire already motivated people and inspire them. People are either motivated or they are not. Unless you give motivated people something to believe in, something bigger than their job to work toward, they will motivate themselves to find a new job and you'll be stuck with whoever's left."

Conclusion

In this chapter, we've looked at some general skills and traits that are frequently listed on job postings for any art-related game development position. These skills are universal for pretty much any development position, but are extremely important for any game artist. In the following chapters, we'll dig into specific art position's required skills and competencies companies look for in candidates.

3

Introduction to Being an Animator

Animators are responsible for giving life to everything that moves in a game. This includes characters, weapons, creatures, and some environmental assets. However, it's not simply applying locomotion to characters, but it's about giving characters personality through that motion and the way they move through their world. In many ways, an animator is an actor who funnels their performance through the characters they work on. Animators will frequently have a mirror or video camera on hand to observe themselves or others performing an action to truly understand all the nuances of a given movement. In cases of nonbipedal work, meaning characters with more or less than two legs, having access to high-resolution animal footage is a must.

An animator will spend most of their time working on characters. This is often because characters require more animation than weapons or environmental assets. For this reason, an animator should have a solid understanding of anatomy, meaning how things move not only from a motion perspective but also from an anatomical perspective. For example, understanding functionally the difference between a socket and a hinge joint and their range of mobility is something every animator should have a grasp of. In addition to a strong understanding of anatomy, any animator should have a solid grasp of the traditional animation principles.

In this chapter, we will be looking at the key skills, responsibilities, and high-level concepts of what it takes to be an animator in the game industry. After that, we'll be looking at some of the basic as well as crucial elements to include in your animation portfolio. In addition to that, there are questions about portfolio and working in the industry posed to some game industry animators. We'll start by looking at the key skills frequently listed on job postings.

Key Skills

- Strong understanding of traditional animation principles and how they apply to 3d
- Able to animate bipedal and nonbipedal characters
- Knowledge of character setup and rigging
- Problem solving and prototyping ability
- Strong game design sensibilities

Interview

What Are Some Key Skills for Working as an Animator?

Steve Madureira: Having a good sense of timing and strong poses is important. A good rule of thumb is to imagine someone could take a screenshot of your animation at any frame, so scrub through and if a pose looks weird even on a nonkey frame, try to clean that up. It'll make the overall animation look better.

Leisel Madureira: A good sense of motion and timing. All principles of motion you learn in 2d can be applied to 3d. Due to the technical nature of games, the ability to quickly adapt to new tools and programs will help you and others on your team as well.

What Are Some of the Tools/Programs That You Use to Perform Your Job?

Steve: 3d Studio Max is the main program that I use. Other useful tools are Outlook for email and a messenger program for talking with other people in the company quickly. Kinovea is a really useful video tool when you capture reference. You can get scripts for working in max too like tools that help you copy and save poses, or mirror animation, etc. The tools I use were written by a good friend and coworker at Vigil Games, Chris Mead.

Leisel: Primarily 3ds max. Maya is more commonly used for animation, in both games and movies, but 3ds max is also common in games and I've only ever encountered max for work. You'll need to learn to work with a studio's design tools to see how your animations play in game.

Depending on how the studio's pipeline works, you might have animators hooking up animations for design.

What Are Some Skills Not Usually Associated with Your Position That Actually Play a Role?

Steve: Knowing scripting or how to work in your game editor goes a long way. It will let you implement things much faster to see your work in game without having to wait for other people to get around to it. Being able to work with others is a big part of the job. I collaborate a lot with designers when working on characters, for example. Another very important thing is being able to take feedback and apply what you hear. If you take things too personal, you will find yourself in a bad mood a lot and also making people not want to talk to you, which makes the job harder.

Leisel: The ability to communicate. Don't know what's needed for an attack? You'll need to talk to a combat designer, or whoever assigned you the task. Is animation not exporting correctly? Are tools broken? You'll want to talk to a technical artist. Is your animation not playing correctly in game and does everything from animation to design look correct? You'll need to talk to a programmer. Even if you don't talk to any of these people directly, you'll do so through a producer and you'll need to know how to explain what is a roadblock so they can relay the information and help you get your job done.

Rigging and Character Setup

Before an animator can start bringing a character to life, the model must be set up for animation. This is often referred to as skeletal or character rigging, or rigging for short (see Figure 3.1). This is the process of laying out the bones and helpers that will allow the character to be animated. After the bones have been set up, ordered, and named correctly, the model will need to be skinned to the skeleton. In the skinning process, the vertices of the model are bound to the bones and weighting is then applied to those vertices. Lower weighting is usually applied to areas around joints where bending occurs during an animation, this is meant to prevent the model from folding in on itself or creating unnatural looking situation on the anatomy. Higher weighting is applied to vertices that are meant to rigidly move with the bone. Most modern programs will attempt to weight vertices automatically to some degree but may require hand tweaking.

While some companies may have a dedicated rigging artist or a technical animator on staff whose specialty is creating the rigs for the game, others expect animators to be able to do this when they receive a model from a character artist. Even companies with a dedicated rigger may expect their animators to have enough knowledge in rigging that they can step in to help the technical animator if they are overwhelmed with work or need to make tweaks to an existing rig. For

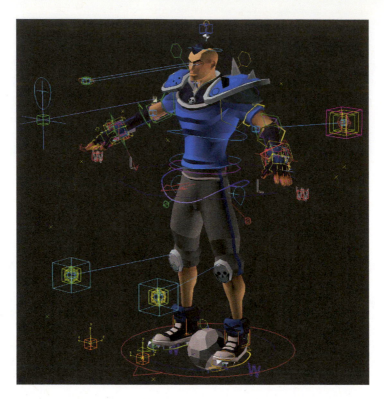

Figure 3.1

This is an example of a human character rig for Super Fuse Ball. (Used with the permission of Gunfire Games.)

these reasons, it's important as an animator to have a good grasp on setting up a character skeleton and having a solid knowledge of weighting as well.

Implementation

Animators will often have a lot of creative freedom when it comes to their work. Animators working on characters will work closely with designers as most of a character's action requests will come from them. Often animators are given a broad brush to paint with when it comes to the particulars of an animation. Designers may require an action to occur in a relative set amount of time or will have a very specific vision in their mind for an action. In these cases, they will give concise direction and requirements that adhere to established game metrics. In either scenario, animators will have a lot of interaction with the character artists and game designers as new animations may need to be added to expand a character's move set (see Figure 3.2). At that point, it's up to the animator to make whatever that action is interesting, believable, and exciting.

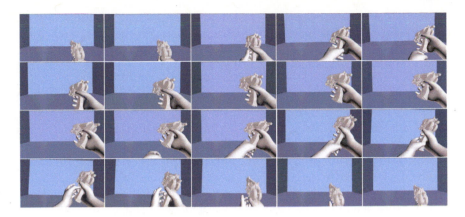

Figure 3.2

Still frames of a reload animation for a first person shooter. Animation by Scott Marshall. (Used with permission of Gunfire Games.)

Depending on the studio, animators may be required to hook up their animations in the game's engine. The tools and engine may be very intuitive or very technical; it all depends on a company's pipeline. Animator's should have some experience getting their work into a game engine as it may be a required part of their job, and at the very least it's good to understand the process. In cases where the animators don't have to hook up their animations, it will often fall to game designers and sometimes to programmers. In these cases, as an animator, it's good to make sure that what you are handing off to someone else is as clean and easy to use as possible. This could range from not having extraneous unwanted frames at the end of an animation to organizing your files before handing them off.

Presentation

While many of the fundamental skills are the same, there is actually quite a difference between how animations are created for a game versus how they are created for a movie or an animated short. In a movie, animations are created much like one would expect them to be; they are produced for a single scene and that animation is played from beginning to the end of that animation. This can include cycles or completely unique locomotion. In games, it's quite different. Animations are produced much more in isolation, a single-run cycle, a single sword swing, or a melee combo are often split out to separate files and then put together in the game editor. Within the editor speed and blending between animations can be manipulated with ease. As mentioned previously, animation implementation will often fall to combat/character designers; however, sometimes this will fall to animators. Some engine's animation systems are quite robust and are similar to digital video editing, allowing the user to link and blend together different animation sets or even layer animations on top of each other. This is a quite different way of thinking of animations as the final animation in Max or Maya may not actually be how it's seen in game.

Problem Solving

Problem solving can come in many forms for an animator; sometimes it comes in the form of a challenging new character, working within tight technical limitations, or even dealing with new or incomplete pipelines. Experience is usually the best teacher in most of these cases, so the more varied characters you work on, the more well-rounded of an animator you will become. In addition to experience, having a positive attitude and a focus on being results orientated when approaching problems will go a long way. For animators, there are a lot of varied and often broken tools out there; knowing your way around these limitations and being able to work with them is the key to staying productive. When new 3d software revisions are released, most of the changes affect the animation tools. Keeping up with the latest updates will help you as an animator to mitigate the time loss of learning new pipelines and working through issues along the way.

In addition to tools, being able to work within technical constraints and platform limitations related to animation is important as well. Different engines and different platforms all have very different specifications and processes when it comes to animation. While it's difficult to learn all of them, it's a good idea to try out a couple different pipelines to get a good grasp of what's out there and what kinds of limits there are in regard to getting animations in a game engine.

Prototyping Abilities

Early in a game's development and even throughout, the need for quick "proxy" animation sets is quite high. "Proxy" is short for approximation, as these animations are meant to be rough but reasonable stand-ins for final animations. This means these animations have the big movements but there is a lack of finish and polish in a final animation. As animator, you will often be expected to supply these proxy animations if the character you are working on is brand new or has new animations not present in other characters. These proxy animations can be utilized by designers to test out early ideas for their designs. The advantage of these proxy animations is they shouldn't take a long time to make, but they let designers try out a character early and in actual game play scenarios as opposed to only on paper. As a designer works with these proxy animations, it allows them to make very informed decisions about the character as well as allowing them to refine a final list of animations needed for the character.

As an animator this means that it's important to be able to quickly get the big movements and timings in for a character before delving into the small details and secondary motion that add personality to the animations. While these are meant to be created quickly, they aren't necessarily throw away work. The final animations should be built upon the template created by the proxy animations. If there is too much change between the proxy and final, the proxy really didn't serve the purpose it was supposed to as any decisions or setup the designer had done based on the proxies won't necessarily be valid any longer.

Strong Game Design Sensibilities

In their own right, every animator is a part game designer. They breathe life in the character models and make a lot of the decisions around timing, mobility, and personality of the characters. Game design for characters is usually quite goal orientated, where the design is often focused on the end goal of what the character does and how they behave. How the character gets there and all the in-between are usually a shared responsibility between the animator and the designer. Game designers focused on characters or combat will be very involved with animators, having a high-level vision for a character's behaviors or have very specific things in mind for a couple of the movements or motion. This can come in the form of a design document or an in-depth conversation with the designer. In many cases, it's up to the animator to take all this information in and apply it in an interesting way to a character. This means finding ways to create personality for the character as well as carry that personality through all the animations. This can be done by paying close attention to consistency of timing and motion cues established early on and maintaining them, and then building upon them through the entire animation set. An example of this is, if there is a large character and it's established in the walk cycle that they are slow and plodding, the rest of the animations should reinforce that established character's direction. In this example, if an attack for this character felt very fast and light with little windup, it would not follow the established personality of this character and would feel out of place. This isn't to say a large character can't have a fast attack, or burst of momentum, however it should still have a nice consistent weight to it.

Additionally, something that naturally occurs as one animates a character is the generation of new ideas as the character is being refined. To really be the most productive with these ideas, it's important to know the goals of the character and its place in game. Animating a character and coming up with a lot of unique and complex animations without knowing it's actually meant to be a minor character can be a waste of time. The opposite is true if a character is hastily animated with little refinement and they are a crucial character in the game. This again goes back to communication skills and understanding the game design goals of a specific character and their place within the game.

In regard to game design and animation, one thing that comes into play frequently when working directly with a combat designer is knowing your frame counts (see Figure 3.3). If you've ever gotten really into a fighting game, you're likely familiar with the concept of counting frames. This idea is very similar to

Figure 3.3

Example of the anatomy of an attack animation. Blue frames represent the windup, green the active, and orange the recovery. Animation by Scott Marshall. (Used with permission of Gunfire Games.)

the process of creating attacks during a game's development. If you're not familiar with the concept, it's that every character in a fighting game or action game has three states to a given attack: windup, active, and recovery. Windup or start-up is when the character would be "building strength" to do the move or often called a "tell" in action games. This is the initiation of the move. In most games, the character is vulnerable during these frames. This is the anticipation portion of the attack. "Active state" is when the attack kicks off and is actually causing damage. In almost all cases, this is the smallest portion of frames in a given attack. The recovery is as the name implies, the character must recover from the attack and is extremely vulnerable during this time. The recovery time in frames is usually dictated by how powerful the move was and how much windup was required. Recovery is usually the longest portion of an attack animation. This is because part of that recovery is returning to their idle or neutral state. The number of frames differs between moves and is often dictated on the power of the move. For example, a quick jab has a short windup of say four frames, short active state of three frames, and short recovery time of five frames, whereas a heavy roundhouse kick might have a relatively long windup of 15 frames, 5 active frames, and a relatively slow recovery time of 20 frames.

Interview

What Does Your Average Day as an Animator Entail?

Steve Madureira: Other than animating, other possible tasks could be rigging and skinning characters. As an animator, I also work closely with other departments like programming and design and spend a good amount of time interacting with them. We are on the tail end of the production pipeline, so we end up being troubleshooters a lot of times when things don't work or look right when they are implemented.

Leisel Madureira: If you have an awesome dedicated rigger, you receive a character ready for animation. Otherwise, you're given a model that you first need to rig (setting it's bone and their motion constraints) and skin it (attaching the model to the bones with a modifier). Once that's done, you're ready to animate your character. You're typically given a list of standard animations, run, walk, idle, combat idle, fidgets, attacks, and transitions to complete. Depending on how complex they are, you'll either dive right in (like for a walk) or draw out/plan a quick and rough "storyboard." You may even record yourself acting out a motion (like for an attack). When animating you'll set your major key frames and once those look solid, you'll break it down with in-between frames. Many artists animate in step key and get all of their major and minor key frames down before turning curves on. Others animate straight ahead, animating the character as you move forward on the timeline without stepping ahead. I typically do a combination of both.

What Advice Would You Give Your Younger Self Starting Out in the Game Industry?

Steve: (Not necessarily to myself since I wouldn't change anything I did since I love where I am right now, but to people trying to get into the industry.)

Try to intern as soon as you can. I learned more from a couple of weeks interning than I did with a year of school. You will learn a lot when you are working in the field and from your peers. I personally think that a bachelor's degree in art is a waste of money. When you apply for a job, they may not even look to see if you have a degree until after they see your demo reel. With animation, it's very easy to show off your skill with your reel. It doesn't matter where or how you learned your skill. If you have skill, you have skill, whether you have a bachelor's, associates, or even no degree at all. You should do as much or as little schooling as you personally require to learn what you need to be able to do your job. You can further hone your skill with tutorials and such online practicing. One thing schooling does offer is peers that are going through the same thing. I would say, I learned a lot more from my peers in school than I did from the actual schooling. I don't regret going to school to learn by any means. I feel like I personally had the right amount of schooling for me. But school is expensive and if you have enough knowledge to intern somewhere, you can learn much faster there and even make money while doing it.

Leisel: Don't be afraid to ask questions. Don't lose hope even when potential employers don't respond. Never stop working on your portfolio. Keep practicing, learn to rig better. Make time to improve. Don't give up because you'll meet some of the best people in your life through work because the people this industry attracts are an awesome, nerdy lot, and you'll feel right at home with them.

Are There Any Misconceptions You Find People Have about Your Line of Work?

Steve: Most people think you sit and play games all day.

Leisel: I don't draw pictures to animate or play games all day. I actually have to make time outside of work to draw and play games. Making a game is not easy or simple. It requires a lot of work from a lot of talented people from many different departments. The idea that if someone isn't happy with the industry, it's easy enough to just make a game themselves. Unless you're skilled and talented in all areas of game development and can afford to not be paid for several months or more, you'll need other people helping you and a lot of resources to fund it.

Conclusion

This should have given you a good idea of some of the responsibilities and competencies that go into being an animator in games. As should be apparent, it's not just making character move. The level of complexity with a given rig as well as the technical hurdles can be quite daunting. Later on in this book, we'll look at what kind of animations one should include and focus on in a portfolio for getting a job doing video game animation.

4

Introduction to Being a Character Artist

Character artists are responsible for the creation of the player characters, creatures, nonplayer characters, sometimes weapons, and even vehicles depending on the scope and size of a given project. These responsibilities can vary from task to task and project to project. Character artists work closely with concept artists and the AD to ensure that their work embody the concept and themes of a given character. They also have a broad understanding of the tools available to them in Zbrush and 3d Studio Max or Maya and how to get the most out of them. A character artist's skill set puts them somewhere between traditional sculptor and fashion designer.

In this chapter, we will be looking at key skills and the core competencies of what is required to be a character artist. We'll look at some of the most commonly listed skills on job postings and examine what they mean. Additionally, we'll pose some questions about being a character artist to some character artists in the game industry. We'll start by examining the key skills frequently listed on job postings.

Key Skills for a Character Artist

- Solid understanding of human and animal anatomy
- Familiarity with different modeling and sculpting software packages
- Keen eye toward form, shape, structure, and silhouette in regard to 3d models
- Sharp eye for light, shade, color, and detail in creating texture maps
- Able to create clothing and equipment, both organic and hard surface.

Interview

What Are Some Key Skills for Working in Character Art?

Brian "Bobo" Jones: Anatomy is the number one skill a character artist must have. Even when making stylized art, an understanding of anatomy will make the art much more believable. You have to know the rules before breaking them!

Adam Pitts: Don't be afraid to iterate early in the process, and get feedback often. Character art is one of the most time-consuming specializations in the field, and, in the game industry, deadlines are everything. Even the most perfect concept art will need changes when executing the actual model—the worst thing you can do is go quiet for 2 weeks working on something that is in the wrong direction of the overall art vision of the game. With the sculpting tools out today, it's easy to whip up several "rough drafts" of a look for a character in little time. Stay visible with what you're working on so there are no surprises for you or the AD as you reach the completion of an asset.

Tohan Kim: I believe one of the most important skills for working in character art is an observation skill. You should be able to analyze, understand, and visualize the completed work in your mind. Further, you need to set the level of detail (LOD) so that you do not waste time on a detail that is unnecessary. It is also important to know where you would put your focus and emphasis on considering camera angle and game play. In order to do this, you also need to communicate well with designers and animators.

What Are Some Skills Not Usually Associated with Your Position That Actually Play a Role?

Brian: Organization. A character isn't finished when the art is done. Before passing it on to other members of the team, you need to make sure everything is clean and easy to pick up by others. Misnaming an object or material can cause issues.

Adam: I would say to anyone getting into game art don't just bury your head in one aspect of the industry. Specialization is fine, but the more you learn about how games are put together, the more efficient you will become at your part, and the more you will be able to contribute to the product as a whole. A quick example—Learning how shaders and materials work can help you when you're planning decals for a character, for instance if you want to add scars, tattoos, makeup, or any other temporary or changeable detail.

Tohan: It is all about team work. As a team, it is very important to have good communication with other departments. When you get the concept, as opposed to doing your work like a machine, it creates a good work environment when you are willing to freely communicate and build good relationships with other team members by sharing ideas and giving feedbacks. This would help the whole team go at the right pace.

Anatomy

Being a good character artist means you have a fantastic understanding of anatomy and form. The believability of a character relies heavily upon the artist's grasp and mastery of anatomy (see Figure 4.1). This requires a good comprehension and application of the natural proportions, musculature, and bone structure. Many character artists refine this skill through figure drawing and gesture sketches with a focus on shape and proportions. With proportions there is a lot of theories and variation on approaches when it comes to different goals on a

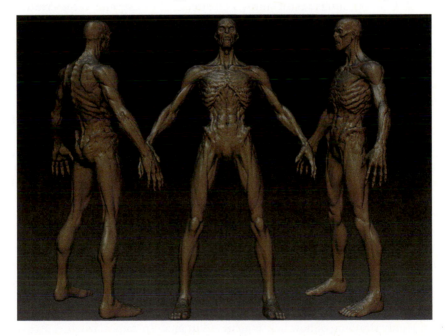

Figure 4.1

Even a *zombie* can benefit for adherence to rules of anatomy. Sculpt by Tohan Kim.

character. An example of this is an average person is 7 and a half heads tall, while an idealized figure is 8 heads tall, and lastly, heroic characters are frequently portrayed as 8 and a half heads tall. This extra length is often distributed in the upper torso and the legs.

Anatomy doesn't just refer to the body, but it also includes the face. The human face, realistic or stylized, is a difficult thing to replicate in 3d. Character artists have a good understanding of the intricacies and nuances commonly found in different ethnicities as well as the traits that differentiate a masculine face from a feminine one. In addition to this, character artists focus on exemplifying or subduing these features in order to achieve a particular goal with a given character. This allows the character artist to add personality and believability to a character. Lastly, understanding how to model a character's face in a rested or neutral position means that the animator will be able to extrapolate a full suite of emotions and expressions from the character's face. Often this goal feels diametrically opposed to the character artist's desire to make a character that has a cool look on their face. For example, building a character with a scowl means it will be quite difficult for an animator to make the character ever look like anything other than a variation of mad. Although a character with a blank look may not be ultimately the coolest a character can look in a portfolio, it is better for the game as a whole.

In addition to the anatomy of a human, character artists need a firm understanding of various types of animal anatomies. Fantasy and sci-fi creatures usually have one or more real-world analogs they are based on. For example, an understanding of how a canine hind limb works would prove extremely useful when working on a werewolf. Additionally, understanding the variation and differences in the skin types found on animals can go a long way to selling the believability. An example of this would be an application of a unique skin like an elephant's skin to a character. In this case, it's not just applying a tiled texture to the character; the skin around joints looks very different compared to how it looks in areas where it hangs loose versus where it is pulled tight.

Understanding anatomy is the first step, but there comes a more technical need to understand how to manipulate and distribute vertices to allow the model to accurately distort when it is animated. Animators or a dedicated rigger will often handle the heavy lifting of the vertex weighting and skinning as well as making sure the model looks good in different poses. It is, however, extremely important for the character artist to build a model that enables the rigger to do this. This means understanding how a body moves. This is achieved by distributing the vertices and edge loops on the model in a way that allows for natural looking deformation and flexing of the implied underlying musculature when it is animated.

While hair technically isn't considered anatomy, it's worth mentioning that a good understanding of how hair is achieved in modern games, whether stylized or realistic, is something every character artist should have. There is a reason why most games over the last decade featured bald male protagonists; hair in real time is hard to do in a convincing manner! Very realistic hair often relies on a lot of setup and specialty shaders to render correctly. This shader setup may be left up to the character artist or they may be provided support. At the very last, character artists will be expected to generate the textures and layout of hair cards on the character. There are a couple of plugins available to assist in this process. Most of the work in the end will rely on the character artist's skills. When it comes to more stylized hair, this will often require less technical setup and rely on the artistic prowess of the individual and their ability to convey hair shape and flow with larger, simpler shapes.

Color, Clothing, and Detail

Color is crucial in any character design. It reinforces the shape and silhouette of the character and allows them to stand out from the environment. Not just any colors can be thrown together, characters are often developed with specific color palettes in mind that not only help them to stand out in their world but also define them as a character. Often key characters will have a color attributed to them that is not used anywhere else in the game to ensure that they are not only iconic but also instantly recognizable anywhere in the game. Color theory plays a large role when it comes to characters. It is essential that every character artist has a firm grasp of color and its application. The same rule found in traditional mediums such as painting or photography is just as applicable to color design of a character in a video game. Often characters will have a very specific palette. Within that palette, colors will often be distributed in an order of dominant, subdominant, and accent. Accent colors will often be a punch of color for a key portion of the wardrobe. It may be the trim of a jacket, a line on a space suit, or an item like scarf. Good use of color distribution is important in realistic as well as stylized games. In fact, it's more important in simplified games as there is often less detail to focus on, and the raw design and color of a character have to do almost all the visual heavy lifting.

Beyond an understanding of color theory, it's extremely important for character artists to understand materials. This means being able to author textures so that metal looks different than cloth which in turn looks different than leather which looks different than flesh (see Figure 4.2). Selling subtle material changes on a character is one of the key elements that separate middle of the road characters from great ones. This understanding not only has to do with how the surface reacts to light, like in the case of its specular response, but also how it shows wear and tear. A simple example of this is how leather shows wear. Treated leather often has a smooth surface except for in areas of wear. Worn leather begins to become rougher and often lighter than the smoother, treated parts. Leather also cracks more in areas where it's forced to bend or twist. Lastly, edges or raised bits of leather will receive more wear than inner surfaces as they are more likely to rub against other objects. This is just a single example, but all materials have their own properties for how they show age and wear.

Figure 4.2

The Crowfather from *Darksiders II*, a character that has elaborate cloth and materials. (Used with the permission of Nordic Games.)

In addition to understanding material surfaces, character artists need to possess an understanding of clothing design, not only of the importance of cloth shape and color, but also how it's worn. When approaching character design, often the most important part beyond nailing the anatomy is nailing the clothing. The clothing can tell a story of a character through its wear, complexity, or even how it's being worn. The wear on a warrior's metal or leather tells the type of warrior they are, for example, how many battles they've seen or how meticulous they are about the upkeep of their armor. The complexity of an outfit can describe the personality and the accoutrements or trinkets may describe their social standing. How it's worn can describe their demeanor or even tell a different story if it doesn't fit quite right. This can go on and on, but much of the character of a character is defined by their clothing.

In addition to clothing design sensibilities, a character artist understands how the clothing is made to some degree, this means understanding where fabric seams fall, how a leather strap fits into armor, where gloves are sewn together, and so on. This means the character artist is partly a fashion designer and also partly a tailor. An understanding of how clothing fits, wrinkles, and wraps over and around the body is just as important to any character design as the character's hair or face. Understanding these things is what allows the character model to feel grounded in their reality with believable details. Even stylized game characters benefit from believably designed garments and armor. Additionally, how clothing is worn, and put together, can help to describe the world the character exists in with a greater detail.

Software Programs

Character artists often use the most programs of any artist on a game team, except for possibly visual effects artists. There are tools specifically for high-poly modeling, low-poly modeling, unwrapping UVs, painting on a 3d model, and burning down high-poly models to low poly. However, knowing this many different programs isn't required for landing a job as a character artist. At a base level, character artists need a fantastic understanding of a generalist 3d program like Maya or 3d Studio Max as well as of a high-poly sculpting package like Zbrush or Mudbox (see Figure 4.3). The reason many character artists use more programs than these two is because often specialist or more focused programs offer a much more robust and reliable toolset.

Figure 4.3

Image of Araxis high-poly sculpt from *Darksiders II* by Tohan Kim. (Used with the permission of Nordic Games.)

Personal preference and workflow also play a large role in determining what tools an artist uses. Much like with any art form, the tools don't make the artist, but they can make the artist more efficient. A good character artist should be skilled enough that they don't have to rely on a large suite of tools just to create a character. Realistically, all the tools that are needed exist within a sculpting package and a general 3d package; however, many of them are lacking the sophistication specialized tools bring to the table. It's worth experimenting with different tools to find out what fits in your workflow and what doesn't. Additionally, new tools are always being released, so it's a good idea to try to stay abreast to the latest software developments relating to characters even if you don't use the tools.

Textures

Creating texture maps has gotten a lot more sophisticated over the years. Very few character artists rely exclusively upon photo textures anymore. In realistic games, they may still be used but much more subtly than 5 years ago. Depending on the workflow and look of the characters, the base texture maps can be generated off of cavity maps, ambient occlusion (AO) maps, or any combination of maps that are rendered out at the time of normal map bakedown (see Figure 4.4).

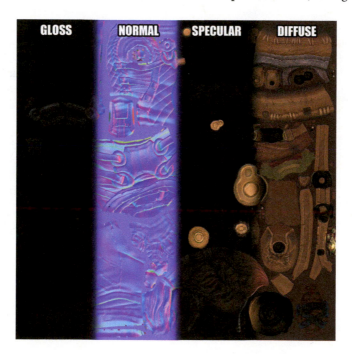

Figure 4.4

Example of the different texture maps used for the character Alya, the Forge Sister, from *Darksiders II*. (Used with the permission of Nordic Games.)

4. Introduction to Being a Character Artist

From here, the character artist has a very accurate starting point for generating the texture. How they are generated from there is entirely decided upon by the style of the characters and the game's art direction.

While just a few years ago, character artists would often paint in highlights and directional shadows and shading into the diffuse maps of a character, due to increased fidelity in real-time AO and lighting, diffuse maps today are often much lower contrast and lack a lot of directional shading. Highly stylized games or ones that run on lower end systems will often need to rely on less sophisticated lighting effects and may still have shadows painted in. Again, every game is different!

Physically Based Materials

There is a movement in games to a more physically based rendering method. The advantage of physically based rendering or physically based shading, the terminology changes depending on the engine, is that materials react to light like their real-world counterparts. What this means is that through proper texture creation and setup, metals, stone, wood, and cloth should react to light the same way they do in the real world. On the rendering side, this is achieved through the application of energy conservation on surfaces as well as a much more accurate representation of Fresnel. Fresnel is the amount of reflection you see on a surface based on the angle it is viewed at. Prior to physically based shading, the brightness of the specular value on the surface was the same value regardless of its reflectivity. This is wrong because as an object's reflectivity of its surface became lower or basically "more diffuse," the brightness of its specular should reduce accordingly. Many engines attempted to get around this problem by giving the artist the option to change the "specular power" per material. While this helped, it still never yielded physically accurate results.

What physically based shading means for a character artist is a slightly different pipeline for texture creation (see Figure 4.5). Physically based shading has

Figure 4.5

An example of a robot character using physically based texture values in a physically based lit scene. Model by Tohan Kim. (Used with the permission of Gunfire Games.)

Figure 4.6

Example of Alya from *Darksiders II: Deathinitive Edition,* a stylized game, benefiting from physically based materials. (Used with the permission of Nordic Games.)

several components when it comes to texturing. First is the diffuse or albedo map. The albedo map is the color of the object with no shading, AO, or lighting information in it. AO is the shadowing that occurs in crevices and recessed sections of an object often caused by indirect lighting. The albedo map should be a relatively low-contrast texture that represents the colors of a surface in white lighting. One exception to this is that shiny or reflective metals should have very dark albedo maps. Some feel they should be absolutely black; however, it depends on the final desired look. Some engines look better with a slight color, albeit quite dark diffuse map for metals.

While some people assume physically based shading is only important or worthwhile for games striving for realism, stylized games can benefit from it too (see Figure 4.6). Physically accurate values help to define a material through its specular and gloss values, regardless of how stylized those textures may be. If they adhere to the predefined rules of physical values, the end result can still be quite visually pleasing in a stylized game.

Process

Character artist's work sits in the art pipeline right between concept and animation. Character work is usually very linear work, assuming there is a good approval process in place. What this means is the concept artist works to produce a final character concept, which is then approved and passed on to the character artist. The character artist then creates that character. There may be points where more concepts are required, or in some cases, the game design of the character changes and the visuals must be updated. After these or any required changes are made and the model has been completed, it is handed over to be rigged and animated by the animation team. At this point, the character artist is done with that character and moves on, assuming the asset doesn't need LODs, color variants, or tweaks for rigging. This is very different from the workflow of an environment artist, for example, who may spend a lot of time going back and forth with different departments and works through a more iterative process to finalize their work.

Interview

What Does Your Average Day as a Character Artist Entail?

Adam Pitts: Zbrush—become intimate with this program. Learning the ins and outs of this program will make or break you as a character artist. At first, this software can seem quite overwhelming, but if you don't master it, you don't stand a chance. Once you overcome its quirks, it's a rather enjoyable experience. Visit their forums regularly for when you need inspiration and motivation as well as tips for workflow—trust me, if you're having a problem with something, someone else out there has also had the same exact issue.

What Advice Would You Give Your Younger Self Starting Out in the Game Industry?

Adam: Be aware that this industry is still very much project based. Studios beef up when in heavy production and thin out after launch. There are plenty of jobs out there, but it is not unusual for guys to have to move every 3–5 years to find a gig.

Tohan: Please focus on growing and learning rather than focusing on your circumstances and weaknesses. Please do not lose your passion.

Are There Any Misconceptions You Find People Have about Your Line of Work?

Brian: The biggest misconception is the speed at which a character can be created. There was once a time when I could complete a character start to finish in 3 days. These characters were 2k polygons and a single 512×512 diffuse map. Now, with current-gen character, they can potentially take up to 2 months to complete, depending on complexity.

Adam: The first thing everyone says is "'oh! What a fun job it must be to play games all day." This could not be further from the truth. To be clear, making art for games is fun, but it's also serious work, and sometimes requires long hours. You will be behind a computer screen for most of your career and from time to time you will be having dinner at the office, get ready!

Conclusion

It should be obvious at this point that a character artist needs to have a deep knowledge of anatomy and fundamental design sense to be a good character artist. Also, great observational skill for proportion and surface detail is a must. A character artist really lives and breathes characters; it's never just a passing interest. Later on in this book, we'll delve into what to include in a character artist portfolio from a content and subject matter perspective.

5

Introduction to Being a Concept Artist

Concept artists are the visual problem solvers on a game development team. What does a visual problem solver do? Concept artists are given a brief description of a task and are expected to take that kernel of an idea and grow it into a fully realized visual representation. Concept artists don't have free reign to craft whatever they want; they will have to work within specific restrictions of a predefined style, mood, and timeline. The images they produce will then act as art direction for the 3d artists on the team to create the in-game visuals. A concept artist's tasks can vary widely from high-level loose environmental sketches to tight, intricate character designs. We'll start by looking at some of these key skills and competencies needed to be a concept artist, and then we'll delve into what these mean and how they are applied to the job. Additionally, we'll hear from some industry professionals with their thoughts about being a concept artist in the games industry.

Key Skills

- Able to explore a wide variety of ideas or styles
- Able to produce final illustration quality work

- Work with a variety of people including those who are not versed in art
- Environment designs that explore a wide range of styles and explore specific moods
- Paintings that demonstrate a wide range of techniques from classical to stylized
- Understanding of composition, color theory, and visual story telling
- Ability to create prop and building designs including developmental sketches

Interview

What Are Some Key Skills for Working as a Concept Artist?

Ryan Gitter: An understanding of design is the biggest thing you need, some people just paint, some people just draw, some concept in 3d, and some do all of it, but without a solid understanding of design and a good sense for storytelling, none of those skills will be good enough.

Christopher J. Anderson: First, know the art fundamentals, and then understand how to research new topics, themes, and turn that info into new visual ideas on a daily basis. It's important to do this in your mind, or on paper in a thumbnail form, to strengthen the ability to dream up visual themes.

Other key skills you need to work as a concept artist varies depending on your skill level, or title. At a junior level, you need fundamental art skills, decent knowledge of the 3d program you will be using, and a modern understanding of concept art ideas and quality bar. You also need to make sure that you have a solid concept process that allows you to get work done on time with consistent, solid results. Your lead or senior should be able to guide you through the rest such as communication between departments.

At a senior level, this depends on the type of concept artist you are. If you're a "category" concept artist, meaning you focus on characters, or environments, or a specific style or genre, then you need to make sure that you stay competitive in that field, even if you are one of the best. You don't want to fall behind and lose your place. You also need to master the art of communication, which is a lifelong journey but getting decent at this will allow you to get better results with your art. Imagine, you can communicate with the producer on why you need certain tasks at certain times, with a certain time frame, or get the AD on board with your idea, or work closely with the 3d art team and designers to help ensure that the quality of your visual ideas is maintained all the way up to getting it into the game. Great communication, especially at a senior level, allows for solid visual ideas that the audience can fully experience.

If you are at a senior level and a full concept artist, meaning that you can perform the tasks of all categories, then the key skills you need are changes. You need to be able to master the art of seeing the big picture of visual design for the product, and help the teams see that vision as the AD approves the direction. This helps the AD maintain a solid vision for the look of the game or film. At this level, you are doing the work of a lead or an assistant visual director. Those titles depend on the company and what's available there.

What Are Some Skills Not Usually Associated with Your Position That Actually Plays a Role?

Ryan: Being able to communicate your ideas verbally, half of your job actually happens in discussions with your coworkers and collaborators. I would say maybe 85% of the time I have a good idea of what I'm going to do before I even start because we've brainstormed it out already.

Chris: Managing upward. Sometimes managers aren't truly sure what they want or how to get it, and it is the concept artist's job to help them. Do this by negotiating and proving how it can be done.

The skill to managing upward is usually something senior concept artists and leads need to focus on more to achieve better communication and workflow. This is not really associated with being a concept artist, but is very important for high-level success in the profession. It means learning how to evaluate, diagnose, and study behavior and mental processes of the people you will directly be working with. By understanding the people you work with, you make it easier to communicate clear info to them, have it received as you said it, and get clear and productive responses back. So for instance, if a manager is the type of person who is too busy to give you crucial information on high priority tasks, and this is a habit that has caused problems, by you understanding the cause of his or her behavior, you can more easily negotiate a solid solution.

Exploration

A large portion of time spent early in a game's development is dedicated to the artistic exploration of ideas at a relatively brisk pace (see Figure 5.1). This earlier point in a game's development is when the ideas are still being worked out and is often referred to as pre-production or sometimes pre-pro for short. This is due to the fact that it should take place before any production of real assets or any final game play has been established. During this time, ideas will be generated, refined, abandoned, and this will be repeated until a direction is established. This process allows for a good amount of iteration to occur and will usually allow the best ideas to rise to the top. From this, a cohesive vision for the game's art will begin to emerge. This time of creation and discovery done by concept artists is the most important part of pre-production for a game, but often is cut short due to budget or scheduling constraints. This can lead to pre-production work for

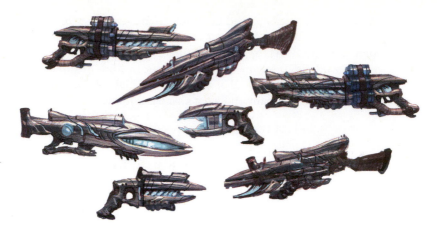

Figure 5.1

An example of alien weapon exploration by Tim McBurnie. (Used with the permission of Gunfire Games.)

concept artists overlapping the start of full production. As a concept artist, it's important to recognize this and be open to large sweeping visual changes during the course of development.

The other portion of time early in the development cycle may be spent taking some of those approved concepts to full-on illustrations where the focus is on the key art which is all about mood, execution, and composition. These illustrations will be used to sell the visual direction and tone of the game to the team and company at large. In these cases, things like functionality and feasibility of ideas take a backseat in favor of generating a beautiful image that people can get excited about. These ideas can then evolve and grow over the course of the game's development, but this gives a good starting point for the rest of the art team.

Concept Art and Illustration

One point that still confuses some people is that concept art is not illustration. However, illustration is a component of concept art; the ability to take a piece of art from conception to a final polished illustration is a vital part of the job. While illustration in itself focuses on the polished execution of a single piece of art, concept art as a whole has the primary focus of refinement and the functionality of ideas. This confusion between the two distinctly different goals is perpetuated by "concept art" shown prior to a game's release or in art books released after a game is finished. Often only polished pieces or "key" art pieces are ever released outside of the studio. This does a great disservice to the work that goes into concept art and the creative thought process behind it. It's key to remember that while the ability to illustrate is essential to being a well-rounded concept artist, it's not the entirety of the work.

At the core of any good illustration are the same elements that are the core of a good piece of concept art—an understanding of perspective, anatomy, framing, and composition. On top of that is the technical ability to render the image to a final state. While traditional illustrators may still use mediums like paints or graphite, most video game concepts artists almost exclusively use digital painting techniques in Photoshop or Painter. The ability to do so requires not only the traditional skills of an illustrator for the application of color and shading but also the added technical skills to really understand how to get the most of your preferred painting program.

Context

The images a concept artist creates not only serve to define the vision of the game, but they also perform a very practical role for the 3d artists on the team. This is why concept artists need to understand how things constructed and how they would function when crafting a concept (see Figure 5.2). In addition to how things work, concept artists need to know their context within the game world. Thinking about the importance of the piece being created in regard to its place in game and visual weight can help to drive esthetic decisions as it is being created. This can run the gambit from creating a key piece of art a player must interact with in a crucial moment in the game to a prop the player will see over and over again. Both of these scenarios have very different visual and game play goals, and the concept artist must take this into consideration when making the concept.

Figure 5.2

Example of a concept that accounts for how the weapon would function and exist in the game world. Concept by Christopher J. Anderson.

Most production concepts remain quite loose, having notes jotted down on them and parts left unfinished if the intent is established elsewhere in the piece. Some concept artists pull reference for materials or shapes directly from real-world examples; in these cases, they will often provide these images in the margins of the concept to help emphasize their ideas.

Communication

In terms of concept art, communication is actually a dual process. It's important to visually communicate ideas through the concepts as well as following up the visuals with verbal communication. Sometimes the goal of a given object, location, or character may not be clear at the beginning and receiving clarity can be achieved by speaking with the artist who will build it in 3d, the designer implementing it, or the AD. This is where having the ability to communicate well comes into play. Often concept artists, production artists, and ADs speak the same "language"; however, sometimes, even between art disciplines, there can be a breakdown of communication. It makes it even more important to keep an open dialog with the artists who will be turning the concepts into 3d assets as well as with the AD to make sure that everyone is on the same page with the goals and objectives of the piece of work.

Outside of the art disciplines, concept artists often have the most contact with the game designers. This is usually where those strong communication skills are needed the most. Designers are more focused on function than artistic aspirations when it comes to levels, characters, weapons, and so on. This doesn't mean that they don't care about the art; in fact, many designers will often craft design ideas off of the concepts that are generated during the course of a game and get very excited to see where concept artists take their initial designs into a full fledged idea. However, as a concept artist, it is important to have a clear understanding of any design functions or limitations when starting a given task. Sometimes this information will be clearly outlined in a design document or it will only exist in a designer's head. Either way, it's important to be in "the know" so that the concepts will be as relevant and functional as they can be. This can also help to eliminate re-work along the way. One thing concept artist need to keep in mind and helps keep their sanity is to maintain a positive attitude even if ideas are changed during the course of development. Often the development of final game ideas and mechanics is a moving target as the ever elusive "fun factor" is often not obvious at the start. Concepts artist like any other game artist will receive feedback to change their work, sometimes dramatically, for the betterment of the game at large.

Visual Story Telling

Visual story telling is often a term associated with film; however, it plays an important role in games as well. In regard to movies, visual story telling often

Figure 5.3

Example of a concept mood piece by Christopher J. Anderson.

refers to the composition of the scene as well as the elements contained within the scene. In film, the scene and its details tell the viewer about a place, character, or an event purely through its visuals. The same is true with games. The composition and elements of a character concept, for example, go a long way in describing their history, personality, and overall feel without the use of any words. The same is true of environments; the details applied to a scene will describe its condition, purpose, location, and more (see Figure 5.3).

As a concept artist, sometimes the back story of a character or location will be provided, while other times, it will be left open. As part of the creative process in creating a concept, it's important to think about the shape language of a given asset, its color makeup, and things like the application of wear and damage. These are just a few of the traits that can help to inform the viewer of the story of a given piece.

Thumbnails

Thumbnails are quick, rough sketches that are really where the concept art process begins (see Figure 5.4). Thumbnails are called thumbnails because they are supposed to be small pieces of art like a thumbnail; functionally, they are quick sketches or doodles to get the initial ideas and design down. They are frequently produced in black and white and focus heavily on silhouette, character, and shape language. Since they are meant to be simple from an execution perspective, the artist has the opportunity to produce lots of them. Sometimes a page of thumbnails will have anywhere from 10 to 30 ideas on it. This is the point where the concept artist has the most freedom and can really let their imagination run

Figure 5.4

Creature thumbnails by Dan Beaulieu. (Used with the permission of Gunfire Games.)

wild. This is what separates a "concept artist" from people who "just like to draw," the sheer amount of designs they are able to quickly generate. The skill of crafting numerous thumbnails really depends on an extensive imagination and an understanding of fundamental design philosophies. It really is creativity and invention at its purest form.

Once the thumbnails are completed, an AD or lead will provide a round of feedback that will either call for more thumbnails or moving onto the next step of the concept process. The next step involves taking the successful elements of the thumbnails and building upon them (see Figure 5.5). This means concentrating

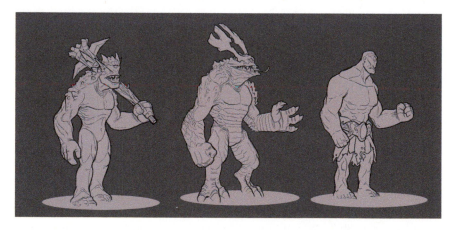

Figure 5.5

Refined creature thumbnails by Dan Beaulieu. (Used with the permission of Gunfire Games.)

on refining the shapes from the thumbnails and defining them by adding detail. Depending on the artist and process, the next stage may be more refined thumbnails, offering more detail on the initial ideas or possibly moving onto a finalized concept.

Interview

What Does Your Average Day as Concept Artist Entail?

Ryan Gitter: Well typically my tasks will last more than a day. If they're smaller things like props or roughs, where I can do multiple images in a day, I'll usually try to keep a balance of having some to work on while I wait for feedback on others. If I have a longer task like a polished environment painting that might take several days, I'll try to send out work in progress updates as I go, maybe twice a day, to my lead or anyone else who might have a say in things.

Christopher J. Anderson: Meeting with the right people for obtaining the correct info to do the task, and then execute. Senior artists tend to have different expectations than new artists within a day, such as managing concept outsourcers and creating high-level concept art that established visual art direction.

For junior- and mid-level concept artists, their day is pretty basic. The lead usually provides the tasks, the time estimates, and will even do the communicating between departments to gather the right information for the task for them. The junior then researches photos of things that will give him or her enough visual knowledge to provide the first pass thumbnails. Then they have that reviewed by the AD. The next few days are spent getting final revisions, and solidifying the final concept. Mid-level concept artists will be given a little more responsibility to communicate with the 3d leads, AD, and designers once in a while as they learn from seniors how to evolve.

What Advice Would You Give Your Younger Self Starting Out in the Game Industry?

Ryan: Learn 3d…that is, Zbrush, Maya, 3ds Max, Modo. It's becoming more and more a part of a lot of concept art, and the results can be pretty amazing.

Chris: Learn how to read people. Knowing the personality types of people allows for better communication and understanding, which ultimately allows for a better product. It would have revealed a few problems that happen to everyone; even to people on very high levels like between ADs and creative directors (CDs), and how those problems can be avoided. For instance, if an AD and a CD are not on the same page about how they desire to accomplish making the game, they will always be at odds with each other. This can cause final art assets having to be redone because the CD changed his or her mind on what they initially wanted. If this becomes a regular problem, it can set back a company's schedule dramatically and miss the deadlines for release dates.

As a concept artist, or a lead, or a producer, and so on, it is very important to learn the people you're working with to avoid the pit falls of weak communication. I would have been able to benefit greatly as a concept artist knowing this early on.

Are There Any Misconceptions You Find People Have about Your Line of Work?

Chris: There are several. One is people tend to confuse illustration with concept art when there is a clear difference, and it is important to know that when hiring concept artists. Many employers assume that concept art is illustration, and so they fall into the trap of hiring illustrators assuming that they are going to produce concept art. They then get frustrated when they can't get the artist to do what they need.

Conclusion

You should now have a better understanding what it means to be a visual problem solver and how much of the game's visuals rely upon the work of the concept artist or concept team. Most assets, characters, locations, weapons, and vehicles must first have a concept before they are created. This means that, as a concept artist, you have a hand in the look and feel of almost every part of the game. A little later in this book, we'll look at preparing a portfolio that will show that you are capable of this and ready for the challenge.

6

Introduction to Being an Environment Artist

Environment artists are responsible for creating all 3d assets that aren't characters in a game. The skill set of an environment artist is probably the most diverse of all art disciplines and can be a catch-all title given to anyone working on 3d art not related directly to characters, visual effects, or animation. However, sometimes even those duties can fall to an environment artist. In most cases, the environment art position can cover all of the following: asset creation, terrain sculpting, texturing, lighting, scene layout, shader creation, technical problem solving, and performance optimization.

In this chapter, we will be looking at the key skills, responsibilities, and high-level concepts of what it takes to be an environment artist in the game industry. First, we'll look at skills frequently listed on job postings. Then we'll delve further into those skills and more as we pose a few questions to our industry interviewees and why those skills are so important.

Key Skills for an Environment Artist

- Understanding of asset creation pipelines and tools
- Eye for light, shade, color, and detail in creating texture maps

- Self-motivation, good communication skills, and a great team-player attitude
- Understanding of form, shape, structure, and silhouette in regard to 3d modeling
- Problem-solving abilities
- Effectively collaborate with game designers and programmers

Interview

What Are Some Key Skills for Working in Environment Art?

Melissa Smith: Environment is one of those departments that require you to wear many different hats. The list usually includes being able to build assets, both unique and modular, sculpting, painting, scene composition, lighting, and intimating the knowledge of the engine you are working in. Every asset you are asked to make may require different approaches. Rarely can you use just one pipeline method for everything; swapping in "the right tool for the right job" will get you far. Problem solving: finding quick solutions, and critically thinking about efficient methods to complete tasks as well as resolving issues within the game. Being an excellent communicator is a pivotal skill. Being able to take criticism and offer suggestions to your AD is obvious, but the environment role is a team effort. You will negotiate with design and other departments on a daily basis to satisfy your artistic intentions and keep the designer's work intact.

Laura Zimmermann: I sincerely believe that having a strong background in art, in general, is very important for any environment artist. Whether its 2d concepts, fine art, illustration, graphic design, architecture design, industrial design, whatever—as long as you have a passion for, and experience in the field of art, that's the most important thing. I've seen environment artists come from many different backgrounds, and they all have unique voices. I also firmly believe that any artist in this industry needs to have a drive to learn new things—not just new programs and game engines, but new methods of doing the things that they've become accustomed to. We're in an industry that's constantly shifting and changing, and all artists have to grow and change with it. A lot also have been said for an environment artist to be able to remain flexible, and to have great communication skills—games are a massively collaborative effort, and we need to be able to work within confines that are set by our peers, as well as challenge those boundaries where possible.

Cory Edwards: To understand environment art, it's also good to understand all the other disciplines that go into making a video game, everything from concept art to level design to programming to production, etc. Knowing the difference between how character art is made versus environment art is important since both jobs use a lot of the same tools and techniques, but are ultimately very different and should be made with different goals in mind. For example, a piece of environment art often employs the use of tiling or repeating textures to achieve a certain look. A character, on the other hand, would go with a much more unique texture.

What Are Some Skills Not Usually Associated with Your Position That Actually Play a Role?

Laura: When I worked on single-player games, I was pleasantly surprised with how much of my story-writing side got to come out and play when it came to the smaller scale of things in games, everything from hand-written notes, coded messages, signage, and advertising— these were areas I was able to have some freedom and really add to the story.

I am also able to let my illustration background get utilized a lot more than I thought I would. I find that having the ability to create my own concepts and carrying them all the way through to in-game assets to be really gratifying. It also helps out the concept artists, when they might be short on man hours.

Cory: Communication. Many people might assume that we spend all our time just sitting in front of a computer all day, but there's actually a great deal of running around talking to different people as part of just about any task. Often there is no substitute for a face-to-face conversation versus email and instant messaging.

Asset Creation Pipeline

This is the creation of assets used in the game; which can vary from everyone's favorite wooden crate (see Figure 6.2) to statues to modular set pieces used to build the levels. Asset creation usually involves high-poly asset creation, low-poly 3d modeling, texture creation, and material setup. This will rely on talents in high-poly 3d sculpting software like Zbrush or Mudbox, 3d modeling software like 3d Studio Max or Maya, and Adobe Photoshop for texture map creation. This is the most basic and easily understood of all duties that are expected of an environment artist.

Along with the creation of assets is the need for an understanding of asset creation pipelines or, in other words, the common practices and workflows used to create the assets, prepping them, and exporting them into a game engine. This means having a solid understanding of completing an asset in 3d Studio Max or Maya, outputting the asset into a game engine and doing whatever setup is necessary in the engine to get the object to show up and function properly. The setup in the engine side could vary from setting up collision to creating a material for it. Different types of objects require different setups. Having a firm grasp of this process is what it means to understand the asset creation pipeline.

Modeling

The ability to model is intrinsic to being a successful environment artist. Almost every environment art position will require you to be capable of modeling as well as to being competent at it. Modeling as an environment artist means that you are capable of crafting a wide variety of environmental objects as well as applying UVs and texturing them. Environmental models often need to adhere more strictly to triangle count constraints than other models like characters, because they are often repeated throughout a given level with some degree of frequency. This means that an over budget or excessive poly count on an object can be more detrimental to a given section of the game than a single over budget key model or character asset.

From a visual standpoint, good attention to detail, silhouette, and thoughtful application of polygons are some of the traits of a good 3d modeler (see Figure 6.1). Attention to detail means thinking of how things are physically constructed as well as how things break down. This runs the gambit of where two pieces of metal would be welded together to where the rust and wear would show up most frequently on a given object. A good silhouette is important to 3d objects, as it helps them to visually define a given space. Crafting an interesting silhouette and the thoughtful application of polygons go hand and hand. Maximizing the polygon budget to give the most interesting possible shape demonstrates that you have

Figure 6.1

Example of an environmental prop by Adam Pitts. (Used with the permission of Nordic Games.)

a firm grasp of how polygons work to define an object. What this means is not wasting polygons or edge loops on long, flat spaces that aren't defining part of the shape. I always refer to this as making the polygons work for you. For example, if you deleted an edge loop on a static environment object and silhouette didn't change, you probably didn't need those polygons.

Attention to Detail Exercise

In this attention to detail exercise, we're going to be looking at probably the most commonly made 3d asset of all: the crate (Figure 6.2). Let's look at some details that can be overlooked that help make a crate more visually interesting.

A. Notice the directional stains. These are caused by water or moisture coming in contact with the nails in the crate causing them to oxidize and darken the water as it rolls over the surface. This is a long and slow process, and adding longer or shorter streaks to your 3d asset can help to describe the age of an item or even its exposure to the elements.

B. Often crates are used for storage or shipping of items as well as to hide health packs in a game. Adding a shipping label or remnants of a shipping label can give a crate a little more purpose and backstory.

Figure 6.2

A well worn crate. A–D focuses on some of the details that make it believable. (Copyright iStock.com/RBOZUKIe. With permission.)

Additionally, adding it slightly off kilter or at an off angle will help to sell the believability of it being a functional item.

C. Notice how each wood is planked as its own pattern and grain. This is because they were most likely produced from different trees, or at different times, or even at different locations. Often when crafting any sort of texture that has wood planks lined up artists will take a single wood texture and overlay the entire row of planks with it and call it a day. Offsetting the wood texture between planks or using entirely different wood textures for each plank can help to sell the realism in a crate.

D. Note how the bottom is darker than the top of the crate. There is a visible gradient here. This is due to the bottom being in contact with the floor and being exposed directly to more dirt and moisture than the top. This is a subtle detail, but thinking about which end something is sitting on and adding dirt or even darkening it will help it to sit in the world better.

Terrain

Terrain creation is different in every game engine (see Figure 6.3). Most of the systems rely on the concept of manipulating the height of a section of geometry that is divided up like a grid and painting textures on that grid. Oftentimes, game editors have their own unique and separate toolset for terrain creation and editing. This toolset can include various brushes for raising/lowering terrain, smoothing terrain, texture painting, and blending textures.

While different engines approach these concepts in different ways, most game engines rely on a simple method behind the scenes: a black-and-white height map

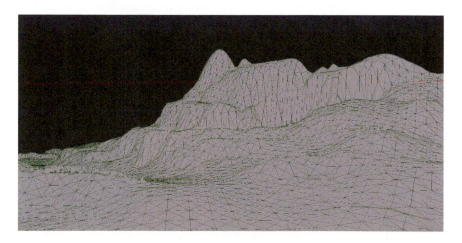

Figure 6.3

Example of terrain in a game engine.

6. Introduction to Being an Environment Artist

and texture masks. The terrain is given visual variety by the use of brushes that raise and lower the geo, where behind the scenes, it is writing out the height map. The complexity of the height map and how it stores the detail varies greatly from engine to engine; however, the end goal is always the same: store vertex location for the terrain in the form of a texture map. When it comes to painting textures onto the terrain, most systems rely on setting a palette, a multimaterial or list of textures to pull from and generating separate masks behind the scenes based on what texture is being painted on the terrain.

Lighting

Lighting is what really sells any scene; it enforces shape and silhouette of the level and can be used as a guide to help a player navigate through the level. Good lighting is also the key to selling the believability of the world. Even stylistic games need to follow general principles of lighting in order to sell their look. Some engines are entirely real time, while others rely upon light map baking to achieve their final results and some do a hybrid approach of the two. In any case, the principles and skill set for lighting are very similar. A strong understanding of color theory, shaders, and application of light is the key tenant of the position. Lighting can mean the difference between a fantastic looking scene and a very mundane one (see Figure 6.4).

Texturing

Texture creation is considered part of the asset creation process, but some studios hire specialty artists who focus entirely on texture work. "Texturing" can be described as the creation of diffuse, specular, gloss, and normal maps for 3d asset (see Figure 6.5). Oftentimes, specialist texture artists are expected to have an outstanding eye for color application, surface detail, a great understanding of how textures are applied to a 3d surface and how they react to light. In cases where it's a position for a texture artist specifically, traditional drawing/painting skills and a strong understanding of UV layout are highly desirable.

(a)   (b)   (c)

Figure 6.4

Example of an underlit scene (a), well-lit scene (b), and an overlit scene (c). The image in the middle demonstrates an ideal value range; there are whites and blacks, but a lot of the asset sits in a middle range. This allows for the surface detail to read really well.

Figure 6.5
One common way to display texture work in a portfolio is to show all the maps overlapped and cross-faded into each other. This allows the viewer to take in all the maps' information easily and how they work relative to each other.

Shader Creation

Not all game engines or even companies expose shader creation control to artists. Some engines have a very robust shader node creation tool, while others have a simplified interface with preset shaders behind the scenes. Some companies purposefully don't expose the shader creation to artists as seemingly simple node connections can have dire consequences on the overall game performance. Still, it's a very valuable skill to have even at a basic level because it really allows you to see how interactions of textures, lighting, and rendering occur in game and how they affect each other. This understanding can allow you to plan your asset creation better and create assets with less guess work.

Performance Optimization

This is definitely a skill that develops with experience, specifically with each game you ship and each game platform you work on. However, there is no reason not to take an interest in this from the beginning. Understanding the strengths and weaknesses of the game engine you are using means less issues later in development. Some general strengths and weaknesses to look for: how does the engine render it's lighting, how does it handle instancing, what are the bottlenecks of the platform you are developing for, how well does it handle multiple draw calls, and how is it at rendering large transparent objects.

Most licensable engines have a lot of tools built in for testing the performance and debugging slow frame rates. In addition to that, there is quite a lot of documentation available online as well when it comes to game performance debugging. Starting out you don't need to be an expert, as mentioned that will come with time; however, having an understanding of these performance indicators early on will help you stand out from the crowd and allow you to make significant contributions to a game.

Interview

What Does Your Average Day as an Environment Artist Entail?

Melissa Smith: I love environment art because I can't say that there is a typical day. Your role is dynamically tied to what phase the project is currently in.

Pre-production: you might be asked to create a set of quick and temporary simple assets that designers can use to rapidly iterate on level design.

Early prototyping: this is the planning phase on how the world comes together. Questions get answered on how you will build your modular sets, what mix of unique props and structural assets will be needed, and what units and shapes work best for quickly assembling the world.

Production: this is the set of tasks most people associate with environment roles. Creating and using a handful of tilable textures to make set pieces and assemble them according to design's needs. Visual story telling through set dressing and composition. Prop creation and lighting as needed late production: 90% of your time will be focused on fixing bugs/problem solving/optimizing. Battles will be fought between art/design/programming, and the game will be wrangled into running smoothly.

Laura Zimmermann: Creative problem solving—both on a large and a small scale. On the large scale of things, I work with the game designers, to make sure that their ideas are being communicated visually, and that the art is helping to support the game play that they have designed. It's also my job to make sure that my art is supporting the larger story of the game and that everything fits visually what the AD would like to see. On the small scale, I make sure that concepts are being represented in 3d how they should, textures are being used properly, that vertices are lining up, all the technicalities; that everything is being represented in-game how I feel it needs to look. Some days I'm talking about the bigger picture with my peers at work, and some days I'm sitting at my desk modeling architecture, or doodling some concepts for some props, or exporting things I've modeled/textured into game—it varies from day to day.

Cory Edwards: Depending on the tasks assigned to me I spend most my time using 3ds Max to model out environment assets, and I use Photoshop to create the textures. There's also a fair amount of time spent researching or discussing with others what they need done for a particular task.

What Advice Would You Give Your Younger Self Starting Out in the Game Industry?

Melissa: Be prepared to make drastic sacrifices. Every studio is prone to closure. No matter how great your job is today, every project can be canceled at any stage and layoffs are eminent. Paired with that, competition is high. So, getting jobs lined up immediately is not always a smooth process. You can't just rely on projects from work to buff your portfolio (especially if that project gets canceled.) The additional personal time and flexibility to move where the projects are will make you a more desirable candidate, but probably a terrible friend/partner. "Normal" things like buying a house or starting a family tend to be options that I consider out of the picture in lieu of my career. Personally, these choices seemed obvious to me. I look forward to going to new places every few years and meeting new people. I also enjoy the steady pressure that forces me to work and get better. I'm very happy to follow the job and move for the right project, but this life style doesn't work for everybody.

Laura: Stay hungry! I think keeping that passion for making games is incredibly difficult to sustain long-term—and you really have to fall in love with whatever game you're making. I've been lucky enough to work on games that I would play myself in my free time, which helps keep up my energy. Looking back, I might not only have given my younger self a bit more of a nudge toward learning 3d early on, but I also would never want to give up my 2d side.

Cory: I don't know that there is a lot I would have told myself. I was very lucky in how I started out and how things turned out over the years. I suppose if anything it might be "Speak up." I didn't learn that until much later in my career.

Are There Any Misconceptions You Find People Have about Your Line of Work?

Melissa: Once you get your big break and some experience, then second and subsequent projects will be easy to hop to. You can relax and you build your portfolio based on studio work. However, you must be continually be sharpening your skills. Competition is constant and never goes away. The level of passion and drive as a community is incredible, but everyone is leveling up at a rate that is impossible to keep up with if you're not practicing regularly. Remaining competitive requires continuing your education throughout your career and working on

6. Introduction to Being an Environment Artist

personal projects after hours. So, when you're not crunching for work, you're typically crunching for personal growth.

Laura: I think that there's a misconception that there's always going to be more of a need for people that are more technically minded, and that art should take a backseat to the technicalities involved when it comes to making games. While I believe that technical knowhow is certainly an asset, I think it's much better to be creatively minded and pick up the technical side along the way. You can teach technical knowhow, but you can't teach someone to be creative.

Cory: Lots of different things come to mind, but most of them are from people who have never touched a video game in their life. For those that have, I think the misconception that what we do is easy. There is a lot of time, effort, and devotion that are put into a game, and it takes a great deal of work to see it through to the end. We don't play video games all day. At least not in the way people might think.

Conclusion

At this point, you should have a solid understanding of the core competencies expected of an environment artist. We'll build upon this knowledge later in this book when we look at creating an environmental art portfolio. While the role of an environment artist can be extremely varied, at this point, you should have a better understanding of what those duties can entail. This should start to form a picture of just what needs to be in a well-rounded environment portfolio.

7

Introduction to Being Technical Artist

"Technical artist" is one of the broadest titles on the art side of game development. Some companies view tech artists exclusively as animation riggers, while others may view them only as Max/Maya/Python scripters. The truth is that it can mean those things in addition to encompassing a wide variety of other skills such as particle creation, shader construction, look development, lighting, pipeline improvement, and performance optimization. Expectations vary greatly from company to company; however, while most companies don't expect tech artists to have all these skills, they'll usually have something in particular in mind when it comes to hiring. Each one of these can be very different skill sets, but they are all categorized underneath the title of "tech artist." It's always important to discuss job responsibilities when interviewing for any position, but it's crucial to understand what a company is looking for when it comes to a TA position.

Key Skills

- Familiarity with MEL, MAXscript, Python, C#, or C++
- Experience working on assets in art different pipelines

- Skills in one or more areas: VFX, animation, lighting, rigging, tool scripting, or shader creation
- Problem-solving/prototyping abilities
- Self-motivated, proactive with good communication skills
- Skills in at least one art discipline: animation, characters, environments, and visual effects

Interview

Can You Talk a Little Bit about the Different Roles a Tech Artist Can Perform?

Ben Cloward: Tech artists are problem solvers. We mostly solve problems for the art team, but sometimes our solutions can help everyone. Luckily for us, there are a lot of problems to solve when working on a game.

Art takes a long time to make and it's challenging to get the art into the game and working correctly, so we build tools that automate tedious processes for the artists, and help them implement the art. Our tools form a bridge that moves their art from creation software to the game engine and hopefully streamlines the process so that the artists can spend their time on making the game look great instead of just getting it to work.

Some TAs focus on graphics. They write shader code that defines the material properties of objects, helps the characters, stand out from the background, and achieves the AD's vision for that game's appearance.

Frequently, there are art tasks that are complex or challenging— like rigging and skinning characters, or setting up cloth simulation parameters. Most artists aren't interested in doing this type of technical work, even though it's still considered to be the art team's responsibility. TAs take on these challenges.

Finally, at many companies, TAs are responsible for the performance of the game. They ensure that the game art is created and implemented efficiently so that the game runs at an acceptable frame rate. They learn what the game engine can handle and educate the artists in techniques for making the art more efficient. They ensure that standards are followed. They troubleshoot problems such as the game is using more memory or running slower than it should. Sometimes they fix things directly and they pass fix recommendation on to the artists or the engineers.

Jeff Hanna: It's hard to limit the definition of a TA. As a group, they accomplish many, many different tasks. A defined TA role at one company could be, and usually is, different from the same role at another company. TAs work as tool programmers, look developers, database managers, communications liaisons, technical support personnel, actual modelers, texture artists, and animators. The most amazing aspect of TAs is how versatile they can be.

7. Introduction to Being Technical Artist

Can You Talk a Little Bit about the Different Roles a Tech Artist Can Perform?

Samuel Tung: TA often plays a key role to bridge the gap between artists and programmers. Needs for TA can vary from studio to studio. For me, a TA should have scripting capability to be hands-on writing tools and help streamlining workflow. The roles that a TA can perform could be categorized as follows:

- General technical artist
- Pipeline technical artist
- Shader technical artist
- Character technical artist (character TD)
- Technical artist for specific assets creation fields, vehicles, environment, etc.

What Does Your Average Day as a Tech Artist Entail?

Ben: The great thing about being a TA is that there are all kinds of things to work on and every day brings new challenges. Each day, I have a main project that I'm focused on. It usually has something to do with improving the graphics or the game's performance. While working on that, I'm often interrupted by artists who have questions about things or need help. I answer their questions and help them out with their needs and then get back to my main project.

Jeff: It varies. I love that it is always different. It will generally be a mix of answering support requests, working on new features for our tools, working on ways to improve the user experience of our tools, and managing our tools and support issues for our overseas outsourcers.

Samuel:

- Communication
- Trouble shooting
- Art profiling
- Tools developing

Scripting

The most common tech artist role is that of a scripter or tool creator. When it comes to scripting, it could involve Python, Lua, MAXscript, MEL script, C#, or even C++. In this role, the TA's primary responsibility is to find ways to improve and refine the pipeline of the entire art team by writing scripts and executables. A key word, when it comes to tech art scripts, is automation. The most common goal of a script or tool a TA can write is to automate or simplify an existing process. This means finding ways to reduce frequent, repetitive processes that artists have to do on a daily basis through the creation of scripts. These can be scripts that run natively in a given 3d program or in an external command line window; ease of use for the artist is key for whatever the method might be (see Figure 7.1).

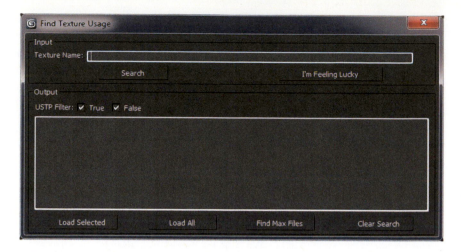

Figure 7.1

Example of a max script created to search for textures within Max files or an entire depot.

The second most common type of TA script is organizational. This can come in the form of creating asset databases, tracking assets, or simplifying the way an asset can be found and modified.

A TA focusing on scripting or programming should share a lot of the same fundamental skills as a programmer: attention to detail, strong math skills, capable of abstraction, and an ability to work within existing code frameworks. Attention to detail comes into play on a number of levels. At a low level, formatting and punctuating are extremely important to pay attention to. But on a higher level, being able to mentally walk through a given portion of code and really understand what it does are equally as important. Strong math skills should be given as all code involves some sort of math; whether it's the most basic addition or complex 3d math, math skills are essential. That's doesn't mean that a TA needs to be a human calculator and instantly knows the answer to any equation, but more that you know how to get the answer. Abstraction in relation to code isn't exactly the same thing as the ability to contemplate abstract thought—a concept that is also important. It's more the focus of breaking down a complex program into smaller parts or subprograms. This allows the programmers or, in this case, the TAs to debug their work a lot easier. These subprograms are different portions of code that can be autonomous functions, or a simplification of this concept: individual "black boxes." Finally, a TA has the ability to work within an existing code framework. This comes into play in regard to working within MAXscript, Maya-Embedded Language (MEL) script, an established tool set, or within someone else's script work. The reason why this is important is because an existing framework often works on some level and a TA may be asked to supplement that framework. Also, if you're working on a team, you will often need to work in a shared code framework. When approaching this it is important to understand what you are looking at and avoid breaking something that previously worked. This is almost the TAs' version of the hippocratic oath, in which they should strive to do no harm or break previously working tools and systems.

When it comes to tools, one sort of common companywide tool is a build process for automatically compiling code, converting art assets, or generating lighting data, and then checking them all into a source control server. Sometimes, these systems can be very robust and offer a lot of information to the team members who use it; other times they are a sort of black box without very good error-reporting systems. A TA focused on scripting will often need to become very familiar with the build process and may be called upon to supplement any existing processes, asset tracking, or even create some error-reporting systems for this build process. To truly understand the ins and outs of a build process, a TA needs to become familiar with all of the company's pipelines and how they interconnect.

Pipelines

A good understanding of art pipelines and the ability to identify and fix weaknesses within them is a talent every TA needs to have. As a TA, being proactive is the best way to improve pipelines. Some pipelines will already be in place when you join a project, so it's important to learn what they do and how they are used. Once you understand the purpose and intent of the pipeline and tools, it's good to begin looking into improving them. The best way to improve tools is to use them yourself as well as speak with the people who use them the most. Speak with the users about issues they have, annoyances, or potential improvements that they have in mind. Once you've done that, you'll be able to approach improving pipelines from a position of familiarity.

From a more technical side, it's important to comprehend what a pipeline is doing to the data as it goes through it and how it stores it. This means, being able to understand what happens to an asset when it gets exported from the core 3d program. What formats do the mesh and animation get converted into? Are they stored in an intermediate format or are they converted directly to the engine's preferred file format? Some engines utilize the universal filmbox or .FBX file format to import data from a 3d program, whereas others rely on a proprietary file type. Having a clear understanding of how to set up a file's model and animations for different file types should be a standard in any TA's skill set.

That covers the basic geometry-related pipeline key points. Now, what happens to the textures in a pipeline? Are they converted to a compressed format by the artist in Photoshop when they save the asset, converted at export time of the 3d asset they are attached to, or are they compressed when they are brought into the game's editor? These are all common methods but they involve completely different pipelines. It's important to understand how all the assets are handled to be able to help debug problems as well as offer improvements to a pipeline.

Shader Creation

Another skill often required in regard to tech art is that of shader creation (see Figure 7.2). Shaders at their core are small computer programs that tell the graphics card how to display visual information. The most common type of shader an artist will encounter is those that interact with artist-created textures which are called pixel shaders. An artist's interaction with pixel shaders can vary greatly depending on the complexity of the engine and tools they use. It could be as simple as assigning their textures in a 3d program, working in a node-based shader creation tool, or even using High-Level Shader Language (HLSL) to create shaders with code.

As a tech artist, it's important to have a good understanding of how shaders are constructed. This relates to shader node creation systems with also having some knowledge of HLSL. Depending on the tools and pipelines available at a given company, a TA may be responsible for creating all the shaders for a game, focusing on unique one off shaders, or perhaps working in a hands-on capacity with a graphics programmer to develop a game's entire shader library. Whatever it might be, having a solid understanding of what is possible, how different looks are achieved through shaders, and how they can be applied to a particular visual problem is a useful skill.

Rigging

Another common definition of a TA is that of a rigger or technical animator. Usually, the job of this person is to cleanly and smartly, often through handwritten scripts, set up the skeletal rigs for the game's characters (see Figure 7.3). Often

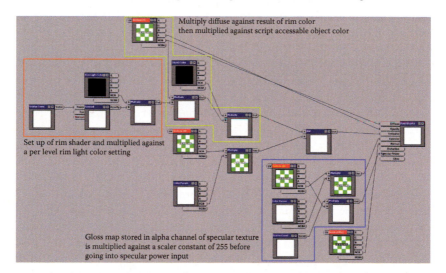

Figure 7.2

Example of a simple shader that has been boxed out to explain its functions.

Figure 7.3

This is an example of a character rig from Super Fuse Ball. (Used with the permission of Gunfire Games.)

a company and its animation team will prefer a particular program, Max or Maya, and a particular pipeline within the program for animation. It helps to have a broad understanding of the different methods available within each program. In addition to maintaining the skeletons for characters, if the company is using any motion capture (mocap) data for its animations, there are support and tools that will need to be created and maintained to handle the large amount of mocap data coming into the studio. Reliance upon good tools and scripts is crucial, as a rigger can quickly become the bottleneck for any animation team when all models need to go through them before they can be animated. The more automation that can be built into the scripts, the more quickly the animation team can start producing animations.

Interview

What Are Some Key Skills for a Rigger?

Chris Mead: First and foremost, a rigger needs to understand animation and how a rig will affect an animator's workflow. A rigger must have strong problem-solving skills. A general understanding of anatomy is also important. It helps to be pretty good at math. They should be comfortable in the scripting language of the 3d software package they are using. A good rigger is a craftsman, paying attention to all the details.

What Does Your Average Day as a Technical Animator Entail?

Chris: Most of the day is spent rigging character models. When not rigging characters, time is spent updating, fixing, or creating scripts and tools. Some of these tools help the animators use the rigs more efficiently, whereas others help to automate repetitive rigging tasks. All work is done to make the animators' jobs easier. A tech animator will also spend time exporting assets and setting up the character in the game engine.

What Are Some of the Tools/Programs That You Use to Perform Your Job?

Chris: A tech animator spends the vast majority of their time working in the 3D software package the animators use. Most studios use either Maya or 3dsMax. If mocap animation is used, Motion Builder is also fairly standard. The tech animator also needs to be able to work in the game engine's editor.

What Are Some Skills Not Usually Associated with Your Position That Actually Play a Role?

Chris: Regardless of an individual's specific job requirements in the gaming industry, it is important to be well rounded with the ability to do other job roles. An animator with modeling, illustration, or technical skills will usually land the job over someone without a broader skill set. As for a skill specific to technical animator, the ability to actually animate is seemingly undervalued by many studios which place more of an emphasis on technical skills. It sounds obvious, but it is critically important to understand how an animator will use a character rig and how to make that rig user-friendly.

Are There Any Misconceptions You Find People Have about Your Line of Work?

Chris: Outside the gaming industry, most people have no concept of what a tech animator does. It's very difficult to explain it, so it's usually not worth an effort. It seems that within our industry many people think a tech animator is much more a programmer than an animator. That may be correct for some, but to really understand the needs of an animator, it helps to be one yourself.

Look Development

This is a unique position and often if a company has never had a TA work in this capacity, it doesn't immediately understand the benefits of the position. While an AD or CD will set the overall vision or style for the game, often times it is in the form of the concept art or a style guide. A TA focused on "look development" would work with the director and art team to achieve this vision in real time. This means visually describing the art style with the application of shaders, lighting, and asset refinement. This is really an artistic research and development position. This position can be useful as unique and complex visual problems arise throughout the development of a game. A TA focused on look development can step in when individuals on a given art team might not have the knowledge or time to dedicate to solving a complex visual problem. Often times TAs can work independently and try out things until they have something that satisfies the technical as well as the artistic requirements.

Lighting

Depending on the company and its art team composition, lighting may actually fall on the TA. This may mean lighting the entire game from scratch or being given a fully lit level that doesn't meet the technical requirements to run at spec. In this case, it's essential for the TA to have a good understanding of lighting both esthetically and technically. Different engines handle the way they achieve their final lighting solution, so it's important to understand the complexities of some of the lighting methods available. This means having an understanding of deferred rendering, forward rendering, hybrid render systems, physically based rendering, image-based lighting, and light map baking systems.

The other side of lighting a TA may be asked to tackle is lighting related to performance. Knowing the strengths and weaknesses as well as a rudimentary understanding of how lighting works will allow a TA to assess a given scene and help tackle performance issues. This will be very important throughout the course of a game's development, but extremely important when the game has reached its final stages.

Problem Solving

While any position in game development requires its fair share of problem solving whether it's actual math problems, visual problem solving, or chasing that elusive fun factor. TAs' primary goal is to identify and solve problems that aren't often obvious or even clearly problems. During the course of development, it's easy for developers to slip into the mode of "if it ain't broke don't fix it." If something is working, regardless of how poorly it is working, there will be little impetus to fix it, as it does what it's supposed to do on some level. This is really where TAs are needed most. In most companies, the programming staff will have supplied a bulk of the tools to get the artists working and have little time to support and improve these tools throughout the course of development. TAs need to be proactive and solution-orientated problem solvers. Often, anyone can point out the problems within a pipeline; however, it's important as a TA to identify how to improve upon the tools and solve those problems.

Another reason why good problem-solving skills are so important is because tools, processes, and programs are constantly changing. Memorizing how a tool works is fine, but it can only get you so far, usually until it's updated. This is where true problem solving and critical thinking are more important than good memorization skills. Extrapolation of previous knowledge as well as the application of that knowledge is where a good TA can stand out amongst their peers. Truly understanding how things work will allow you to better understand why and how they break or stop working.

Communication

Communication comes up in this book a lot. That's because it is important for every game developer. In relation to the position of a TA, it is a good portion of the actual time spent on the job. Having the ability to communicate with multiple disciplines and understand their needs and concerns will only help to improve a project. At many companies, there is some sort of divide between artists and programmers. This is where the TA must act a bridge between the disciplines, or, at least, a point of contact for either side.

From the art side, the TA needs to understand the concerns and issues of the art team on the project. With this information, the TA needs to be able to identify key issues and address the ones they are capable of solving either through scripting, tutorials, look development, or any other means at their disposal. However, there can be issues that are too big or beyond the skill set of the TA that may require support from the programming team. This is one of the crucial times when communication skills and knowledge of the pipelines heavily come into play. The TA needs to be able to take the feedback from the artists and distill the information down to its core; from this, they should be able to make a concise list of requests or improvements. At times, it's helpful for the programming team if the TA can include some examples of how it could work from an interface perspective or integration standpoint to help it fit into the existing pipelines. Programmers who craft the tools that artists use don't typically use them after they have finished writing them. This means that they might not fully comprehend how the end user is actually using the tools. How does the user use interface with the tool? How frequently do they use it? Are the results always predictable? Any of such information ends up being extremely useful for the programmer who ends up working on the tool, and all such information can be provided by the TA.

New tools aren't always the top priority for a tool team or a game company. They also want to make sure that the tools they have work as intended. Tool problems can be hard to track down unless they are flat out crashing all the time for everyone on the team. There can be strange reproduction steps needed to expose a bug or issue. When a bug is found, a TA will need to work out the actual steps to reproduce a bug and provide a "repro" or reproduction case for a programmer. They then use these repro steps as a test case to fix the issue in question. Again this relies heavily upon the TA's knowledge of the pipelines and their ability to communicate.

The other side of this communication bridge is taking information from the programming team to the artists. TAs end up being the guinea pigs for any new tool or pipelines, so they can end up having a rather intimate knowledge of how a tool works and can also offer insightful feedback during a tool's creation. Due to this intimate knowledge and early hands-on time with new tools, TAs can be expected to teach an art team how to use a new tool. This can come in the form of a live presentation, a Wiki page, official documentation, or a detailed email. All these are common and accepted forms of communication and are expected of a TA. The second part of this communication and actually the most important part are the follow-up and support to the initial release of the information. TAs should periodically check in with the users of a tool to make sure that it is working as intended and as close to what they expect as possible.

Attention to Detail

As with any art position, attention to detail is very important. We briefly touched on attention to detail in regard to scripting; however, it also plays an important role in regard to the art side as well. One of the ways this comes up for a TA is when they need to do visual comparisons. Often TAs will be tasked to look into new tools, compression methods, or entirely new systems before they are distributed to the team at large. A TA will be responsible for examining and identifying any minute differences between the old system and the new one. This could come in the form of a new texture compression algorithm where the TAs may have to do a/b comparisons between two textures, identifying any differences, and documenting them. Another example may be a new file format or compression system for 3d models. In this case, they'll need to pay close attention to things such as smoothing group translations, welding, and vertex ordering. Additionally, there could be a new animation compression system and the TA may need to do numerous tests to see what the most optimal quality versus file size setting is.

New systems aren't the only time this attention to detail comes up; older systems usually have many undiscovered bugs or nuances that aren't always known or exposed to all. Learning a system or pipeline and what its expected results are when a 3d object goes through it requires a keen eye. This can come up most often when training a new artist on the pipeline or when the team is starting a new project or attempting a new process.

Finally, an attention to detail is important when viewing the game you are working on. Things such as inverted normal maps, missing textures, vertex problems, skin weight issues, or color discrepancies can be missed by most people viewing the game on a daily basis. A TA should be conscious of these things and frequently keep an eye on the game to help to head off any problems.

Beyond a visual attention to detail, a TA needs to have a thoughtful attention to detail when writing documentation on tools or pipelines. TAs are the ones charged with supporting and maintaining art tool documentation for a project as they usually have the most intimate knowledge about them. Good documentation means assuming that the reader of the document has no prior knowledge of the tool or system that is being documented. This is the best approach to take because often times the individuals using the documentation the most are new team members or outsourcers. Good documentation needs to be clear and well prepared. Users will frequently scan through it or use it as reference when they need it. Knowing this, the documentation should have good organization with headings and a clean layout. Pictures are also very important for two reasons. Those using the documentation the most will be artists and artists prefer visual documentation to long drawn out text descriptions. Also, pictures are very useful because the reader can compare the document's picture and what they see on their screen very easily, allowing them to move through the process quicker. Another trait of good documentation is having the foresight to think of possible questions that may arise and preemptively answering them directly in the document. Finally, keeping your documentation up to date is possibly the most important component of all. A document that is not up to date is sometimes worse than no documentation because it can be frustrating to the reader.

Skills in Another Discipline

In most cases, artists aren't expected to have skills in other disciplines; however, in tech art for some companies, there can be this expectation. There can be many reasons a company looks for this; however, we'll hit on the major ones here. First, companies look for expertise in another discipline because they understand the value of experience. A person who has done a particular type of work will always have a better perspective on how to improve the workflows and systems than an outside observer ever will. Having done animation means you will have a better understanding for creating a rig or animation-specific scripts than a nonanimator. Having experience with environment art means that you understand where the time is spent and where the greatest time saving tools can be applied. Basically, it's assumed that you will know and understand the day-to-day workload and where pipeline problems may lay.

Another reason for skills in another discipline is because there may be dry spells in the workload of a TA or the workload in another discipline may be more pressing. There can be days or weeks where there are no high priority tasks for the TA to work on, while there may be a big deliverable that requires extra hands-on animation or environment work, for example. In these cases, a company may look to a TA to supplement a specific team, either in a hands-on capacity or in dedication of support. In an ideal world and team structure, this should never be a concern. However, schedules can change and priorities can shift. What this means is that a TA should always be proactive looking to improve tools and making longer term pipeline plans. Not every company is ready to dedicate resources to a long-term tool or a pipeline plan; however, it's good to think about it because there may be smaller, easier wins in a long-term plan that could be implemented sooner than later.

Performance

For the bulk of the development time on a game, the TA acts in a key role of supporting content makers; however, there's a point in any game's development where content creation slows and the focus turns to making the game run reliably. Some companies choose to throw everything in the game and improve performance at the very end by globally reducing things such as high-resolution texture, complex shaders, and polygons in a large, sweeping pass, whereas others like to manage the performance during the entirety of the project, reducing surprises at the end. Either way, a TA can be proactive, familiarizing themselves with the assets going in the game, design aspirations, and systems of the game early on.

Performance is a tough yet rewarding task to delve into. Open world, exploration-driven games, and 60 frames per second linear shooters have very different technical aspirations. Assets, lighting, and level construction need to be coordinated and built to achieve these different end results. This is one of the areas that few artists enjoy or really grasp how they can affect positive change. If things are built smartly and with some conservatism, polygons won't be the biggest frame-rate detractor. Shaders, draw calls, light size, and fill rate are often the bigger frame-rate killers. This is where a TA looking at a scene or level as a whole can make more informed recommendations on true performance impactors. Getting to know the tools, platform, and pipeline of the art team is a fundamental to being successful in this capacity.

Interview

What Are Some Skills Not Usually Associated with Tech Art That Actually Play a Role in Your Job?

Ben Cloward: Patience and humility are "skills" that every TA should have. Problems arise and things go wrong and TAs are responsible to fix them. If you let your pride get in the way of getting the job done, you won't get very far.

TAs also have to have a knack for trouble-shooting issues. You have to be able to break down a problem into simple elements and check each one to find the source of the issue.

Jeff Hanna: People are generally surprised when I tell them that the three strongest skills a TA needs to possess are communication, problem solving, and critical thinking. People tend to think that strong programming skills and knowledge of art creation tools would be the most important. But TAs are primarily problem solvers and communication enablers. Being able to identify and solve a problem, and communicate the issues and solutions to others are vitally important to being a good TA.

Samuel Tung:

- External development: I have been helping with streamlining outsourcing processes since my first job in activision.
- Web developing: I designed and developed a web-based asset management system.
- Database administration.

What Are Some of the Tools/Programs That You Use to Perform Your Job?

Ben: The artists use 3dsMax and Maya, so I have to know how to use them well enough to solve any problems that might come up. Most of the work I do in Max and Maya is scripting in MEL, Python, and MaxScript. We also use Photoshop. I spend a lot of time using Text Editors for editing scripts. I also spend a large amount of time in our game engine.

Jeff: We write almost all of our own game development technology, so my main tools are Wing IDE and Visual Studio for Python and C++ coding. I also use Perforce for source and asset control, 3dsMax, Maya, and Motion Builder for art creation. And, of course, Outlook for email communications.

Samuel:

- Notepad++, I just keep this open
- Python, QT, IDE: PyCharm
- 3D package: 3dsMax, Maya
- Photoshop

Are There Any Misconceptions You Find People Have about Your Line of Work?

Ben: A lot of people think that making video games is the same as playing video games. When I tell them that I make video games for a living, they think that I just sit around and play all day. This couldn't be further from the truth. Making games requires deep thinking, problem solving, determination, and a lot of hard work.

Conclusion

Now, it should be apparent why the TA title can be considered broad in its definition and scope. Most TAs aren't expected to fill all of these roles; however, there is often an overlap in some of the roles and a TA will need to be knowledgeable in at least a few. When considering TA as a career, it's important to understand your own strengths and pursue the focuses accordingly. Later in this book, we'll look at how to prepare a portfolio for several of the different TA focuses.

8

Introduction to Being a User Interface Artist

A UI artist or UI artist's responsibilities can differ from company to company. Some companies will have a dedicated UI team where responsibilities are broken up along discipline lines; others rely on 1 or 2 individuals to do the entire UI system. Even the title itself can come with different responsibilities depending on the company. In some companies, the UI artist will only be responsible for generating the art for the UI. This means all icons, life bars, power meters, and tutorial-related art. While at some companies they are much more focused on the flow and end-user experience using the UI. Yet at other companies the UI artist is responsible for both and in some cases even some of the programming or scripting. A UI artist at their core is a graphic designer; they must be able to communicate and solve problems through the use of imagery and typography. In addition to this, other skillsets include layout, flow design, and concept art creation. We'll start out by looking at some of the high-level skills a UI artist must possess. After that we'll delve into some specifics that should be included in every UI portfolio as well as hear from a professional UI artist.

Key Skills

- Designing, prototyping, and implementing UI experiences
- Comprehensive knowledge of layout design
- Proficiency in Adobe Photoshop and Flash
- Excellent grasp of typography and color theory
- Strong understanding of UI usability principles

Interview

What Does the Term "User Interface" Actually Mean in Regards to a Game?

Mike Nicholson: The definition varies from studio to studio, but in a nutshell, UI encapsulates everything from the look of the buttons and menu style to the way the game feels when playing/interacting with it.

How Would Describe What a UI Artist/Designer Does?

Mike: I see the role of the UI person to serve as the intermediary between the designers and the players. It's our goal to translate complex design systems into easy-to-digest interactive elements for the end user.

What Is the Overall Workflow for Creating the UI or a Portion of it for a Game?

Mike: Pipelines vary from studio to studio but generally speaking the first stage is that design has a system that needs to be implemented. Sometimes they can provide a detailed wireframe breakdown of the flow they want while other times they may only have a rough concept to work from. A good UI professional can accommodate either end of the spectrum.

UI Experience

UI experience actually describes two different related concepts often abbreviated as UI and UX, user interface and user experience, respectively. These are related but have different implications. UI, in regard to games, often refers to the controls and interface elements like maps, inventory, and menus that the player directly interacts with (see Figure 8.1). UX refers, as its name implies, to the experience the player has with those interfaces. This is where intuitive design and navigation flow come into play. The goal of any UI is to present the vital information to the player without slowing down or getting in the way of the overall game experience. These elements need to be clear and obvious without bogging down the screen or the player with a lot of information.

The UX focuses on the quality of the experience in regard to how the player is able to successfully navigate the UI elements in the game. The flow of the experience should be logical and never ask the user to blindly navigate into submenus or to a place they are not expecting. UI involves the use of thoughtful imagery,

8. Introduction to Being a User Interface Artist

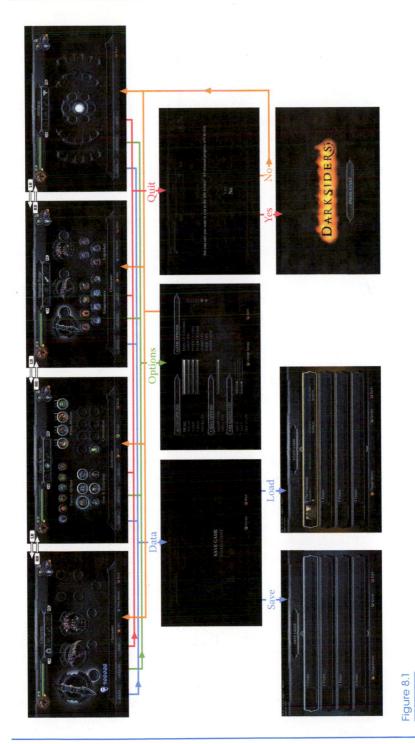

Figure 8.1

Example of the flow and player experience in the UI in *Darksiders*. (Used with the permission of Nordic Games.)

iconography, color, and some text to guide the player through a game's menus, systems, and inventory. This guidance shouldn't require heavy hand holding and should build upon a visual and logical rule set throughout the game. For this reason, consistency of visual elements and cues are at the core of a good UX. The goal of any UX is that the player is engaged and an active participant in the experience.

To succeed at allowing the player to have an active role, it's important that the player has a clear idea of what and where the interactions are. For example in an inventory menu it should be obvious what parts of the screen the player can interact with, which parts are there for visual flavor, and what parts are there to inform the player. The player should never try to interact with the weapon descriptions if they are meant to be passive elements in the menu, and if it is meant to be interacted with, it should be obvious at a glance. Additionally, the use of color and choice of how to draw attention to the important elements within the UI are also important parts of the overall UX.

Another key conceit of a positive UX is to build upon established touchstones and rulesets. This allows a UI to cater to the user's expectations and allows for faster immersion into a given system. Some examples of this are button assignments present in many games. Depending on the game system the user is playing on, in any given menu "accept" is almost always assigned to the A or X button while the B or Circle button is set to "cancel." This consistency allows the UI/UX artist to play into a user's previous experience and expectations right off the bat. In some cases, the console manufacturers actually dictate the look and size of the buttons on screen as well as some of the functions within the menus. They do this because they realize the importance of consistency in the end user's experience.

Layout Design

Layout design in games is somewhat similar to web design layout in regard to the emphasis being placed on functionality, consistency, and ease of navigation. Functionality means above all else it has to work and be well-suited to its intended purpose. Whether the end goal of a portion of the UI is to inform, to allow upgrades, to allow navigation of the world, or to just save the game, the UI has to allow the player to do this with some ease (see Figure 8.2). Consistency means there is a consistent visual language and a level of conformity between all elements present in the UI. This could mean the elements of how the player views their health, currency, or stats are presented in a similar format throughout the UI. Ease of navigation should always be the top priority and often comes with nailing the functionality and consistency. As mentioned earlier, the player should never be asked to take a blind leap into an area of the navigation. Areas should be labeled clearly and categorized well and in a way that is logical to the game itself. The player should be able to find what they are looking for easily, without a lot of guess work.

Creating a UI that is easy to use can be broken down into a couple of key concepts. The first and foremost is keeping it simple. The best UIs often won't be remembered because they were basically invisible and did exactly what was

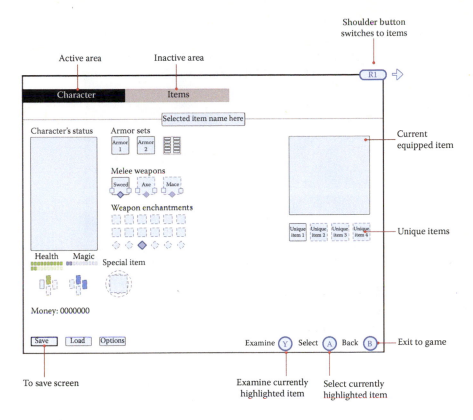

Figure 8.2

Example of a character equipment interface layout.

expected of them. Any time there are elements that can't be simplified; a good UI will help the player to make the logical connections either through building on the use of other UI elements or with a concise tutorial. The repetition of simple and familiar elements throughout a UI will act as these building blocks for the end user to extrapolate upon. These elements can become familiar to the user through use of color, text, or repetition. Strategic and consistent use of colors throughout a UI will help the player to make those logical connections to unfamiliar parts of the UI. Lastly is feedback to the user. This means when they use a health potion, level up a weapon, choose a new perk, or change a setting they are given proper feedback for the action. The end user shouldn't interact with something in the UI only to be left wondering, "What did that just do?"

Conceptualization

Early in the inception of a game's interface, a UI artist may be required to provide mockups of the entire experience through the UI before creating any actual

Figure 8.3

An example of the progression of the merchant screen from *Darksiders* through early concept to final implementation. (Used with the permission of Nordic Games.)

art (see Figure 8.3). This means how the player navigates the menus to get into the game, how the player navigates the pause menu or inventory, and how they receive important information. Some tools commonly used for this prototyping phase are Visio, Photoshop, After Effects, or Flash. The key early on and throughout the entire process is ensuring the highest level of usability as well as the playability of the experience.

Often the UI artist will need to work closely with the game director, design director, or producer. This varies depending on who holds the vision of the game and has a high-level understanding of the systems and mechanics within the game. From there the UI artist can generate navigational flow ideas with an understanding of what the important elements of the game are. In a shooting-focused game the reticle, player health, and ammo are going to be the most important elements on the screen. While a role-playing game will likely need to focus on elements to clue the player in on situational awareness such as their party member's status, the enemy's health, player's health, and energy/mana pool.

Another important element that is thought about but not always settled upon in the conceptualization phase is the dynamic display of elements. What I am referring to are elements that may not be always present in the player's heads up display (HUD), but show up in specific scenarios. An example of this is in a first-person shooter when the player is hit there is often a red directional arrow. That is meant to inform the player of the direction they are receiving damage from. This arrow isn't always visible because it only makes sense to show up in the context of the player taking damage. Another example is early on in a game some HUD elements may not be present because they aren't available to the player at that point. The interface will need to account for the space and location of those elements when they show up later. It would make for a very bad user experience if the player started a game with a health bar in a specific location but later received a mana bar that forced the health bar to move to a different location in the HUD. This is why UI artists need to understand a game and all its systems to make informed decisions when they craft a UI.

Prototype

Once a sound and functional UI has been designed, the next stage is to prototype the approved design (see Figure 8.4). This can occur in game, in flash, or even after effects. The aim is for prototype to be interactive. The goal is to work out usability and flow issues that may not have been apparent in the early stages of the design. This is very similar to putting together the framework for a website

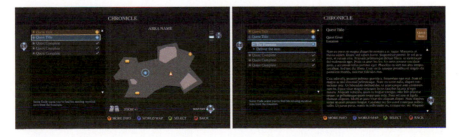

Figure 8.4

Example of early *Darksiders II* quest log UI prototype. (Used with the permission of Nordic Games.)

before introducing actual content. Before progressing to the art creation stage, if this is in a good working state, the UI design will be shared with other people on the team to get their usability feedback experiences with it. Oftentimes things that weren't obvious problems can become very apparent at this point.

From this point the UI artist, possibly with hands-on help from the concept team or AD, will begin exploring the visual style of the UI. UI artists must always walk the line of quick readability, ascetically pleasing and complementary to the game's overall style. An example is if there are icons for weapons in the HUD and the player enters the pause menu, there should be a consistency between the two menus and the game at large that allows the player to easily identify the weapons in these multiple scenarios. They can be identical or at the very least they need to be similar enough to not cause confusion. In regard to a pure interface perspective, simple things like the A button moving the player forward in one menu while exiting out in another menu is very confusing from a usability standpoint.

UI artists usually have the support of a programmer or multiple programmers to implement their UI into game; however, in some cases the artists are expected to implement their work into the game themselves. It doesn't hurt to ask during an interview where your responsibilities would lay and what kind of structure is in place for developing and integrating the UI. It's better to not get the job, than to take it and realize you are incapable of handling the work.

Interview

What Advice Would You Give Your Younger Self Starting Out in the Game Industry?

Mike Nicholson: Be patient, and don't get emotionally involved in anything you do. As an artist it's very easy to get emotionally attached to something you create. However, when it comes to UI, usability trumps all. It can be a difficult pill to swallow when you've created what you feel is a beautiful interface only to have to tear it all down when usability testing reveals it's failing. Oftentimes the less esthetically pleasing layout option proves to be the most successful with regard to usability.

Are There Any Misconceptions You Find People Have about Your Line of Work?

Mike: I don't think that people understand all the thought processes that go into an interface design. From choice of font to the color of a button, trust me when I tell you that there have been at least a dozen meetings where heated arguments have discussed everything you see.

What Are the Things You Would Have Liked to Know about Your Profession before You Started?

Mike: UI is possibly the most contentious part of the game. It's judged by every standard as the rest of the game's contents, but also with the added

8. Introduction to Being a User Interface Artist

pressure of usability. People are shockingly opinionated on UI as it pertains to their personal taste which means feedback is oftentimes volatile and passionate in equal measure. It can be tricky navigating the feedback without coming across as defensive or standoffish.

Conclusion

This is a brief overview of what a UI artist does as well as what's expected of them. So much of a UI artist's job is focused on refinement and revision based on feedback. It's important to approach UI work with a thick skin and an open mind as major portions of a UI may need to be redesigned or completely scraped late in a game's development. This means being able to work fast and change direction quickly is a desired trait in a UI artist. Later we'll look at how a UI artist can prepare a portfolio that allows them to demonstrate the skills and competencies we've looked at here.

9

Introduction to Being a Visual Effects Artist

Visual effects artists, or VFX artists, are responsible for creating all of the particles and VFX in a game. Particle systems are animation simulations of very small sprites or textures that are used to represent a wide variety of visuals from smoke to explosions to waterfalls to weapons fire. These and other visuals use particles because they are very difficult to represent exclusively through 3d models or other methods. The scope of responsibilities of a VFX artist can vary widely from project to project and can include such things as character attack effects, fire and water related systems, weapon particles, magic spells, and not so obvious things like post-process screen effects, particle driven creatures, sky domes, and shader creation.

In this chapter, we'll be looking at the responsibilities of a VFX artist in the games industry. In Chapter 17, we'll examine some key elements to include in a VFX portfolio. In addition to that, there are questions about working in the industry posed to some game industry VFX artists. We'll start by looking at the key skills frequently listed on job postings.

Key Skills

- Experience creating particle systems and VFX
- Experience creating and using shaders
- Understanding of timing and traditional animation principles
- Strong Photoshop skills for creating textures for use in particle systems
- Ability to quickly iterate, and implement feedback
- Excellent communication skills

Interview

What Are Some Key Skills for Working in Visual Effects?

Jay Bakke: Since VFX are simulations generated by collection of numbers and variables, it creates a steep learning curve; understanding how the numbers play off each other is the key. This is the biggest place I have seen artists struggle, trying to make the transition from another discipline to VFX. It is really easy to drastically alter the look of an effect by even the slightest adjustment of a number. Take the time to learn what each number does, one at a time, so that you set a visual target in your mind and predictably arrive at the look you expect.

Having an eye for timing is important so a background in animation helps a lot. This is especially significant in a combat focused game where character animations only span a few frames. Traditional animation principles like anticipation and follow through still apply for VFX. For example, a magic flame punch will have a charge up effect (anticipation), a fire blast effect (motion), and some lingering turbulent embers or smoke (follow through).

Understanding the basics of shader manipulation (UV distortion, displacement, Fresnel, etc.) will give you a big leg up as well, since VFX editors are getting more and more complex in this area.

Ryan Rosanky: VFX is sort of an all-around problem-solving job. "We have this big aurora borealis type thing we want in the sky" and with that, it's your job to figure out the best way to make that happen. You have particles, meshes, shaders, and a lot of other tools in your tool belt and need to know how to use them all to make the cheapest and best looking VFX possible.

What Are Some Skills Not Usually Associated with Your Position That Actually Play a Role?

Jay: There is a lot of engine work VFX artists have to do with scripts and databases in order to get a creature or an event setup with effects. You may even need to setup a custom scenario where you can test out these effects. For example, if there is a scene were something crashes through a wall, you'll want to strip out everything you don't need and set up a custom script that will play that sequence out in a loop. You don't want to play through the entire level every time you make a minor change. Quick iteration is super important to an effects artist.

Ryan: A very important part of a VFX artist's job is to understand the game in its entirety. Talking to level art and animation as well as character design all play a role in how your effects help tell the story and blend into the world that the team is trying to create.

Particle Systems

As mentioned above, particle systems are a unique element in games as they are used to solve visual problems not solvable through just models and textures. Visual effects can include geometry and aren't necessarily limited to lots of small 2 triangle planes. Often particles have their own tools in an engine that allow the artist to modify and change elements over time. For this reason, particles systems are very dynamic and a good eye for timing is crucial when it comes to creating them. A particle system itself often relies on an emitter as its point of origin and a number of parameters to describe how and when things should occur for the visual effect. Some examples of these parameters include decay rate, gravity, color, speed, scrolling, as well as a number of rendering mode options.

Particle creation often requires a base level if not a solid understanding of different rendering methods and when to use them. Some examples of this are knowing when to use opaque, blend, additive blend, alpha test, lit, unlit, or any combination of these (see Figure 9.1). While you don't have to understand how

FIGURE 9.1

An example of a VFX explosion utilizing a number of different blend modes in its different components.

the rendering occurs in code, it is important to understand how the different rendering modes work visually. This is just as important as knowing when to use multiply versus overlay in Photoshop. For example, in the case of Photoshop, they both allow you to introduce transparency of one layer to reveal the underneath layers, but how they do it and the visual end result are very different. The same goes for using different blend modes with particles. Blend, or in some engines translucency, takes a constant value pushed through the shader or from a texture sample to determine an object's transparency value. In additive blend's case, it takes the pixels and adds their value to any pixels behind it. This means it never darkens the pixels, and can only make pixels brighter. This effect is similar to the different "dodge" layer options in Photoshop.

Shaders

In addition to having a basic understanding how rendering in real time works, having a good comprehension of how shaders work is particularly essential (see Figure 9.2). Much like understanding how to get the most out of the different render modes, shader creation, and modification is also important to getting the most out of your particles. Many engines allow the VFX artist to create and modify existing shaders. The capacity to understand how shaders are built and how shader node networks function are extremely important skills of a VFX artist. While some companies don't have access to a shader node system or only allow programmers to create shaders, it's still important for VFX artists to understand the way shaders are made so they can make informed decisions in regard to particles. Being able to build upon that core understanding and think outside of the box are both extremely vital when creating VFX because oftentimes the best effects are built through experimentation.

Animation

Visual effects are very similar to traditional animation in the sense that a lot of the same principles apply: squash and stretch, anticipation, secondary action, timing, and exaggeration. Visual effects artists utilize these principles to sell believability and readability of their VFX systems. Applying these principles really makes the effects come to life to describe the tactile nature of the effects and to a larger extent, the game world. Understanding the principles of timing and weight is extremely important in creating convincing effects. Effects that hang around too long or don't dissipate as expected make for a bad visual experience. The weight or specifically the gravity settings on a system are extremely important to selling the density of a visual effect. For example, if there are multiple components to an effect like a ground explosion, the rock geometry spawned off the effect needs its own weight to look like believable rocks while the smoke should dissipate and float off. If the smoke and rock had the same weight

Figure 9.2

An example of a particle system utilizing six different components for its final visual result: Samael's Portal from *Darksiders II*. (Used with the permission of Nordic Games.)

values, it would look very strange and unbelievable either due to falling smoke or floating rocks.

Fundamentals like timing and anticipation are core to selling any visual effect. Anticipation comes into play with things like fuses, rockets, or really anything that can trigger a secondary element. For example, finding the right timing to sell the buildup of the detonation of a grenade and the follow through of the actual explosion is crucial to selling the experience to the player. If the buildup is too short, the player won't feel anticipation before the explosion, or if it's too slow the player might actually forget about it and get distracted by something else. Often timings like these will come down to the game design, but the VFX artist can have an impact on selling these timing cues.

In addition to having a firm grasp on the principles of animation, often VFX artists will work directly with the animation team on the project to apply effects to characters. Understanding how characters are animated both in general and for a specific project will inform the VFX artist of how to set up character effects and how to attach them a character. Most character VFX are attached to specific character bones or the VFX artist requests what can be called a "null" or dummy bone to attach their effects to. This "null" bone doesn't end up driving any visuals on the character model itself, but acts as a location for the effect to spawn off of. The reason for this is that the bone animates with the skeleton of the character; however, since it doesn't actually drive the character's motion its orientation and size don't matter. Some engines allow for "nodes" to attach to the skeleton and this can act in the same way as the dummy bone and is actually a bit easier since it's not an actual bone tied into the skeleton and its location can be adjusted after the fact a lot easier than a bone can. Both are completely valid ways of attaching effects to a character.

Tools and Time

A VFX artist must find ways to get the most out of the least in terms of tools and time. Aside from the licensable game engines out there, most proprietary engines are light on the VFX tools. This means VFX artists need to be creative with not only their art but also how they produce it. Learning the ins and outs of a couple of different engine's particle tools will give you an idea of how different engines attempt to solve the same problems. For example, creating flipbook textures, rendering out sprites, and how to get that working in an engine can vary dramatically in different tools sets.

Also, due to the nature of how VFX are applied in game, VFX artists are usually at the end of any pipeline. They're often the last artist to work on something before it goes into game, which means on one side they have the nonmovable milestone date, and on the other they have everyone else eating into their time. This is where VFX artists must find ways to do the most with the little time they have. Every VFX artist handles this differently. Working in a highly iterative, proactive way will alleviate some of these "rock and hard place" scenarios.

All game developers should make it a priority to be good at managing their time. VFX artists in particular need to be very good at this, because as mentioned they are at the tail end of almost every pipeline. Some ways VFX artists handle this is to preemptively create placeholder effects. If they are proactive and seek out information on the status of assets they will be working with later, they can plan accordingly. They can begin to prototype some visuals and get creative signoff from the leadership early on, so when they are actually ready to work on an asset they can hit the ground running.

Textures

Textures are at the heart of every particle system. The sprites that make up an effect are nothing more than polygonal planes with textures on them. These textures can be still images or animated frames that are called flipbooks. Flipbooks are much like the name implies, a grouping of still images that when played in quick succession appear to be in motion. There are many tools and programs out there that allow VFX artists to create flipbooks. Many 3d programs allow for the output of renders of flipbook images natively while some engines support the creation of flipbooks inside them by allowing the user to create sequentially numbered images.

At the core of being a VFX artist is a solid understanding of Photoshop and the crafting of textures within it as well as an understanding how to create alpha masks. Often alpha masks are just as important as the RGB layers of a VFX texture. A poorly crafted alpha mask can break believability of a particle effect or just make it look bad. For example, an image of fire on a black background with a poorly crafted alpha mask will likely show the black outline around the fire, leaving an undesirable final visual effect. A VFX artist will be expected to hand paint, render out or manipulate existing images in Photoshop to create the basis for their particle systems. Understanding the importance of a proper resolution as well as readability in a texture is an important skillset that will often come with time. However, even a VFX artist just starting out should pay attention to these elements. A VFX system should look "right" in its environment no matter what in regard to its size, weight, resolution, and physical attributes.

Atmosphere

Visual effects artists often have the biggest impact on the atmosphere of the game (see Figure 9.3). The way a level is built and lit often can portray a particular

Figure 9.3

Example of a scene from *Darksiders II: Deathinitive Edition* without and with VFX. The addition of VFX can do some much in regard to setting the mood, atmosphere, and movement to a scene. (Used with the permission of Nordic Games.)

mood and esthetic, however, VFX often dictate the atmosphere and ambient movement of the game world. Weather, fog, smoke, fire, sparks, and water are all types of visual effects, a VFX artist can place to create a specific atmospheric feeling and add ambient movement to a scene. Careful placement is an art when it comes to creating an atmosphere as it should not detract from the scene either visually or even technically, in the case of lowering the frame rate due to too many effects. It is a balancing act of applying the right amount in a scene to feel natural, for whatever the world is, without beating the player over the head with too much.

Since VFX artists are one of the last artists to touch a level, so they have a unique opportunity to see the level in a near final state and make informed decisions on where the VFX can have the most impact and work to enhance what is already in the level. This allows the VFX artist to reinforce existing visual themes in a level and really sell the world as a cohesive place instead of just a collection of assets.

Math

Programmers aren't the only developers that have to deal with math on a daily basis. Artists often have to deal with very different components of math, and VFX artists are no different. The most common forms of math for a VFX artist is color math as well as algebra and geometry. Visual effects artists spend a lot of time working with RGBA values: 0–255 values that represent red, green, blue, and alpha. Some VFX systems and engines have very robust color manipulators and color pickers while others require the artist to enter in actual RGBA values by hand. In either case, it's important to have a good understanding of how the color inputs are used to affect particles.

Some VFX systems don't require a lot of color information in their base texture and rely more on value than color variance. In these cases VFX artists will create what is sometimes called a combo map. This technique uses each channel of an RGBA texture as an independent black and white, 8-bit image, allowing the VFX to save on memory and texture reads. What this can do is allow the VFX artist to pull distortion maps as well as the base texture image in a single texture. An example would be using the Red channel as the mask for color intensity, the green channel the distortion texture, and the blue channel for the texture that will be used in rotation. This sort of specialized combo map system is highly dependent on a system that allows the artist to have full access to the shader parameters.

RGBA values aren't always used exclusively to drive color. In some systems and shaders, VFX artists will use RGBA values or even RGBA channels in a texture to pass numeric values through for a particle system. If this sounds confusing, think of it this way: RGBA values represent colors but they are still numbers and even in a texture each pixel is storing a numeric value. If a shader is set up in a particular way, it can use those numeric values for math. Shaders can have direct input values, for example, a shader can have a node in it that passes a value of 0.5 through. However, if a VFX artist wants to pass something through that's a little bit more random and chaotic than a single fixed value they can pass through an image to introduce an organic feel.

The simplest explanation of this would be applying distortion to a texture. In this case we are looking at distortion of a single texture, not full-screen distortion, which is a similar post-process effect but handled in a different way. In the case of distortion of a texture, all that is occurring in the UV data of the base texture is being manipulated. A simple way to do this at a per-pixel level is to create a cloud texture in Photoshop consisting of red and green clouds. What this is actually doing is creating a different 0–255 black and white cloud image in the red and green channels. In the shader, the U-channel would be set up to take input from the red channel of the cloud texture while the V channel would take input from the green. The visual result would push the U location of the pixels in the reddest parts the furthest and the least in the areas lacking red. The same would occur to the V where the green is applied. If you then took this cloud texture and added a UV scroll to it, those red and green pixels would constantly be moving and affecting every pixel of the base texture differently every frame.

Communication

Every position at a game company requires "excellent communication skills"; however, we'll look at why it's important in regard to a VFX artist. Communication for a VFX artist is critical to their success and sanity. Asking questions early and truly understanding high-level goals of a task allows them to prototype and begin thinking about possible solutions early in the creative process. Also speaking with character artists and animators as an asset is being worked on, means getting VFX nodes in early that will allow the VFX artist to begin prototyping right away. Lastly, priorities can quickly change so it's a good idea to speak with designers and animators frequently about a task as priorities may slip or change completely without much notice. These are examples of taking a proactive role on a team as opposed to a more passive stance where work is just being delegated to them. Being proactive in any game development position is crucial to one's career and growth as a developer.

Interview

What Does Your Average Day as a VFX Artist Entail?

Jay Bakke: At Bungie, I work in a large team of VFX artists so we all have our own specializations. I typically work on effects for combatants (monsters) and special operations (large/custom/unique events like boss fights and unique story events). For combatant effects, the tasks are typically short, often paired with some database work for implantation, and will require working with a combat designer. For special operation effects, the tasks may take several days to finish, are often paired with complex scripting, and will require working with several people spanning multiple departments.

Ryan Rosanky: An average day includes a LOT of tweaking values, color, and movement of particles to get exactly the timing and feel you want in your effect. The day also includes a lot of communication with other departments. Spending time with design can make your job a whole lot more fun and engaging. If you are into an idea and fully understand what design is trying to convey to the player, chances are you will have tons of ideas on how to achieve it.

What Are the Things You Would Have Liked to Know about Your Profession before You Started?

Ryan: I would have loved to have had a better understanding of shaders, a good understanding of game design/progression, more modeling, and animation experience.

What Advice Would You Give Your Younger Self Starting Out in the Game Industry?

Jay: Think twice about trying to get into the more saturated markets like character modeling and animation. VFX is a complex and rewarding position that has been in high demand for quite a while. Had I learned earlier that explosions, lighting, and blood VFX in games was an actual career choice, it would have lead me to focus toward it right away.

Don't expect landing your first job to be an easy road. You really have to make your own luck by unrelenting persistence. Get yourself to the "right place" and pay attention to find that illusive "right time" then make it happen.

Ryan: Work hard. Enjoy the chance that you have been given. Know that you have the opportunity to change technology and lead visuals in games …. What more do you want? Pay attention to the artists around you grow and be inspired by the massive amount of creativity this industry has.

Conclusion

As we've seen, VFX artists need to be quite technical and have a good sense of animation fundamentals. Additionally a good understanding of color and its application are important as well. Visual effects artists get to have a hand in almost every part of the art in a game, which can be a daunting task at times. Later on we'll look at what kind of samples should be included in a VFX portfolio.

General Portfolio Theory and Application

Portfolio Theory

Now that we've established the general skills and responsibilities for some of the art jobs found in video games, we'll look some of the general concepts and theories behind building a strong portfolio. This section primarily focuses on principles to keep in mind when you begin assembling your portfolio and setting up your site. This will cover universal ideas and are applicable to any of the art disciplines. In later chapters, we will delve more into the specifics of tailoring a portfolio to a particular career path. We'll also hear from some industry professionals, who have spent a lot of time leading art teams as well as reviewing portfolios.

Interview

What Are Some Key Items That Are Must-Haves in a Portfolio for a Game Artist?

Patrick Ingoldsby: When it comes to games it's keen if your examples not only demonstrate quality skill but also have examples of technical understanding. For example, offer a ghosted wireframe that shows clean topology on a model. And occasionally show well laid out UV page samples. We are after all engineering art for real-time rendering engines.

Take the time to show your examples with good rendered lighting. There are very good options available for artists to help showcase their hard work and raise the presentational quality. Rendering software like Marmoset Toolbag or the latest Unreal Engine offers powerful and effective ways to output your pieces. Be sure to study recommended lighting setup tutorials and keep it simple. Too many lights aren't always easy to work with.

Most importantly the best portfolios demonstrate passion. Ambition becomes clear when the quality of the work represents all the time and hard work an artist invested in their own personal development. Becoming a strong games artist doesn't happen overnight. It's a lifetime of art practice, dedication, and your joy of learning. The best artists challenge themselves and never stop learning. This is the perfect industry for that!

Keith Self-Ballard: You must have work in your portfolio that is relevant to the studio to which you are applying. If you use an all-fantasy portfolio to apply for a position at a studio known for doing games in a sci-fi setting, they're just going to ignore you. Do your research. Develop a style and build a portfolio that demonstrates assets that look like they could integrate straight into that studio's style or franchise.

What Are the Most Common Mistakes You See in a Portfolio?

Patrick: I have a tough time with pieces that lack clarity with what the candidate contributed in them. If you have a "team-based" example in your presentation I would advise proving guidance so we'll know exactly what assets or efforts are particularly yours. Directors and leads certainly appreciate demonstration of collaborative team-based work but have a tough time judging your personal skill when "what" you did is not pointed out.

Another would be "don't show more than you have to." If you're not the strongest traditional artist but your 3d is strong, omit the weak traditional art. Many game artists are highly skilled at generating amazing assets without being strong at concept illustrations. Stick to examples that best represent your strengths only. For the sake of a quality presentation, "When in doubt, keep it out."

Keith: The most common mistake is building a portfolio that is too broad. One character. One environment. Two props. One VFX Shot. A portfolio that lacks focus or fails to clearly identify a core aptitude will consistently lose out to the portfolio that demonstrates focus in a key discipline and mastery over of the core principles related to that discipline. Unless you are applying to a very small studio, one where the expectations are that each person is capable in multiple areas, generalists have a very difficult time finding work.

I also dislike blog-style portfolios online. Blogs are organized by time, rather than by type of content. If the candidate's most recent piece isn't as good, it's still the first one a prospective employer is going to see. If you like having a blog, keep it. However, create a portfolio site separately for job applications.

Variety

From indie games to downloadable games to phone games to AAA console games, today there is more variety in games both from a gameplay standpoint and from an art perspective than any other time in gaming. This runs the gamut from 2d retro pixel art based games to complex, visually realistic games to completely unique virtual reality experiences. As an artist, this means you need to show you are versatile and adaptable to different visual styles. You don't need to represent every possible style out there; however, it's good to show you are capable of producing a couple of different styles and not limited to a singular look in your work. This isn't always possible with school projects and deadlines, but it is important to make it a priority as it shows your depth and versatility as an artist.

In addition to styles, it's a great idea to attempt different subject matter especially if it's outside of your typical comfort zone. This could mean anything from fantasy to modern day to sci-fi to historical done in any particular look from heavy stylization to photo realistic. Having good variety in your portfolio and showing that you can tackle a range of subject matter and styles with confidence can go a long way to describing your flexibility as an artist. If you struggle to think of subject matter, take some cues from modern games. Look at their worlds, their characters, their visual effects, their UI, and how things move through the game world. This should act as a great inspiration for what kind of things to put in your portfolio that is both current and relevant.

Focus

One thing to keep in mind is unless a studio is very small, art generalists aren't in as high of demand as they once were. This means when thinking about variety it's better to stay within a specific discipline or field like character art, environment art, concept art, etc. than attempting one piece from each. Having a portfolio with a multiple types of work in it often doesn't show very well. This also means that you have had to split your time and focus, and may leave you with a very limited perspective on the different disciplines. This will often hurt your output as people who have chosen a particular path have been able to delve deeper into it and this will often yield them much stronger results. This doesn't mean you have to pick a direction when you start out and stay the course all the way through until you get a job. You should explore the different art disciplines to find out which suits you best. Find what you are most drawn to and refine that skillset. Your portfolio should reflect a specific focus that shows you have a clear understanding of the position as well as how to do the work.

Narrowing down your art to a specific focus shouldn't feel limiting; it's actually quite the opposite. Keep in mind that there is a lot of variety to be explored in a given field and attempting to have something from every field waters down your focus. Every piece you work on should be a learning experience that makes the next piece you do even better than the previous. At that point you are building upon a knowledge base from your previous work. The more work you do within a discipline, the stronger that base becomes. Again, spreading yourself out doing a single concept, a single environment, a single animation, etc. means you don't have that strong foundation to cultivate.

Presentation

How you present your work speaks volumes about you as an artist. A good presentation shows a high level of professionalism and commitment to your work (see Figure 10.1). This means good lighting for objects, clean wireframes, and smooth transitions or cuts in videos. In regard to still images, it's important to arrange pieces in an esthetically pleasing way on the page. Having a border theme or template for your work that carries across your portfolio is a good way to unify everything. If you're struggling for inspiration in this department, have a look at some of the commercially available industry art books: *Gears of War*, *God of War*, *Uncharted*, *Assassin's Creed*, *Darksiders*, etc. While you shouldn't steal from them directly, you should strive for that level of presentation. After all, the end goal here is that the artists in these books will be your peers 1 day.

FIGURE 10.1

Example of a clean, readable presentation of Zbrush Assets by Adam Pitts. (Used with the permission of Nordic Games.)

10. General Portfolio Theory and Application

Figure 10.2

An example of a good character presentation. The focus is whole character but the included close up shots really show the detail found in the character. *Beliel* by Tohan Kim. (Used with the permission of Nordic Games.)

When it comes to presenting 3d assets, having good lighting is a must (see Figure 10.2). While it may not be your biggest strength, every 3d artist should know the basics of lighting in 3d and setting up a scene with good lighting. This can mean setting up light rigs in a 3d modeling package and outputting renders. It could also mean importing your 3d assets into a game engine and taking your screen shots there. Either way lighting is so important. I really can't stress enough that lighting can make the difference between a mediocre screenshot and a fantastic one. This is especially true with making modern assets. Most modern assets will have a diffuse map, specular map, normal map, and maybe even a specular mask or gloss map. All those textures rely on lighting to "work." A diffuse map sometimes called an albedo map relies on lighting to define the diffused color of the object. A normal map depends on lighting direction information to apply the surface detail, and the specular map and mask depend on lighting information to describe the surface's shininess and reflectivity. With poor lighting, you're doing a great disservice to your asset and all the work you've put into these individual maps.

Portfolio Navigation

This goes hand and hand with presentation; however, this is more about the actual navigation of your site and how people interact with it. There are a lot of hosting options out there: Squarespace, Wix, Wordpress, Blogspot, DeviantArt, Tumblr, etc. It doesn't matter if you go with a service that has built in templates or if you design it from scratch, the only thing that truly matters is ease of viewing for the end user. Some site types are better than others; in particular blog type sites have distinct advantages and disadvantages. These sites can be great because they offer a chronological look at all of your work and often a viewer can see the evolution of a piece and its refinement. However, the flipside is that the format of these sites can become a distraction. If there is anything posted besides your work like thoughts on restaurants, what you did the previous weekend, or pictures of your breakfast it fails at being a useful portfolio tool. With a blog type format, you may be tempted to post doodles and other nonfinal work that doesn't show well without the proper context. Also, if it is a site that displays images of your favorite artists or recommended links on the page it can be detrimental as well. The last thing you want is someone going to your portfolio to see your cool art and getting distracted by a preview of some else's cool art. That isn't to say blog sites can't be used for your portfolio; however, go into it with the intent of posting only portfolio level content, suppress the distraction content common to blogs, and it can work well.

Simplicity of design trumps all (see Figure 10.3). Overly complex interfaces and flashy navigation will only get in the way of what people are there to see: your art work. From a design and layout perspective, if you're not a UI artist don't make your portfolio your first foray into UI design. A straightforward, cleanly designed site will let your work speak for itself. There is nothing worse than your

Figure 10.3

Example of a very simple, straight forward portfolio layout with easy navigation. The sections are readable tabs at the top, art contributions to the actual image are outlined at the bottom and there are thumbnails of the rest of the images from the current section. (Used with the permission of Nordic Games.)

10. General Portfolio Theory and Application

Figure 10.4

Avoid this at all costs.

website format getting in the way of the content of your portfolio. Keep your navigation simple, and the images as accessible as possible.

When you lay out your portfolio, sometimes you can be too close to it and may not see the flaws in the presentation. Just as it is important to seek feedback with the content of your portfolio, it's also crucial to get navigation feedback of your actual site. Is it easy to view all the work? Were there too many subcategories? Did everything load correctly? This doesn't need to be an extensive process, but it's good to get other eyes on it. Remember that people reviewing your portfolio don't have a lot of time and want to see your work right away. Long flash introduction animations or images that take a long time to load should be avoided at all costs.

Another item to avoid is relying on nonstandard plugins to view your work (see Figure 10.4). There are a lot of really cool and crazy plugins used to display 3d work in a browser; however, that doesn't mean you should use them. Often, you never know what platform or browser an individual will be viewing your portfolio on. Often it will be on a PC; however, smartphones and tablets are sometimes the choice as they are more convenient for busy reviewers. On PC alone there are at least three major browsers and some plugins aren't available for all of them. Also, consider that even if the plugin is available some people do not want to download them because they can often be bundled with unwanted software. The point of all this is that your portfolio needs to be accessible as you can make it to all platforms and users.

Group Projects

Many game school art programs have an emphasis on team projects, whether it's a final project or thesis project; it will usually be part of the curriculum. A lot of them attempt to model the groups after somewhat realistic game team structures. Having the experience and work to show from a team project is great and demonstrates you can work with peers to accomplish a larger goal than you could achieve on your own. It's a good step toward working on a game team and learning to collaborate with others. The key to including a group project in your portfolio is clearly labeling your work and contributions to that project. Sometimes, artists will include images from a group project with no context for what they actually worked on for the project. Be clear and upfront about what you worked on by calling out elements or parts in the given piece of work.

As I mentioned, some schools will attempt to mimic a game team structure. This includes putting people in positions like "Art Director" or "Producer" or "Creative Director" for a group project, which can be a great learning experience. However, the unfortunate thing about this is that it can sometimes mean the participants had very little experience doing the hands-on work for the project. This translates to having nothing solid to show in their portfolio. If you worked on specific things, animations, lighting, VFX, textures, models, concepts, UI, be sure to call them out. Putting images from a school project where you served in a supervisory role doesn't really impress anyone outside of the class room. Chances are you're applying for an entry level job where those skills won't be what the company is looking for; they most likely want production artists that will be producing content. What this means is it's often better to opt out of the "glamourous" lead positions to get more time to focus on asset creation.

Criticism

Every artist should strive to grow and expand their skills and abilities. One way to experience that growth is through critique. The first lesson any production artist must learn is the ability to take critique. Critique and criticism can be positive or negative; however, hopefully it is constructive. The point of exposing your work to critique is to get feedback that comes from someone who is removed or not attached to the art as much as you are. This can be peers, teachers, or even online forums. Once you do, remember that sometimes your first reaction might be to feel defensive. However, there is no reason to feel the need to defend yourself; allow the criticism to come unfettered. After it has been given, it is your choice what you do with it. You can choose to ignore it, or react to it by making changes to your work. Often inexperienced artists feel that critique from a lead or an art director is an attack on them personally; this is largely because they see no separation between their work and themselves. As an artist working on a game, you need to realize that it is no longer "your" work as it contributes to a much larger goal; a finished game. This is an important stage of growth every game artist needs to realize at some point. Critique is not a personal attack, and your work is not you. Once you are working for a company, you are using your skills to craft someone else's vision which you may not always agree with. Learn to take criticism in stride and grow from it, don't fight it.

Prior to getting a job, and even after getting one, peer feedback is a great place to get initial feedback for any piece of work. Peers can offer insight from a similar but slightly different perspective. Peers may be doing similar but not exactly the same work as you oftentimes and can see your work from a "distance." They can offer artistic feedback as well as technical feedback or offer up alternative creation methods. As any game artist will tell you, most of their learning was done while on the job and it was probably from their peers. If you have the opportunity to be in a 3d class, seek feedback from your classmates regularly. This can help you to not only improve your work but also get used to receiving critiques.

In addition to in-person critiques, another great place to get feedback is online 3d forums. However, having access to so many different places to display your work, it's easy to get overwhelmed with the feedback. Also like most social interactions on the Internet much of the posting is done anonymously. This is exceptionally bad when attempting to receive consistent feedback from posting your work. Unless you are a regular on that forum already, you probably have no idea who is posting or their ability to critique. That's why it's still usually better to get feedback in person if it's available because you have some context for the opinion. An example of understanding the context in feedback: if your professor loves classic sci-fi and they give you critiques that are trying to move a piece of work toward that classic sci-fi look, you can understand the bias and apply the feedback as you see appropriate. However on forum, you often have no context for where the feedback is coming from or why.

There are, however, some unique advantages to posting on a forum as opposed to in person feedback. One such advantage is the chance to gather a "consensus." What this means is you may receive the same specific critique from multiple sources, and if this is happening you usually should address whatever keeps coming up as it's likely a valid point. Think about getting critique from multiple people almost like a focus group. If a couple of people hone in on a specific thing about your work, you can assume that in a larger sampling of viewers you will receive the same response. However, also be careful as this notion can fall apart on forum critiques where people can agree with someone even if they don't have a valid point. They can agree with someone because they like that person. Sometimes this can end up being more akin to noise than something actually useful.

Self-Critique

Now that we've gone over critique from others, we need to look inward. Being able to objectively look at your own work, filter out the weaker pieces or pinpoint weak parts of a piece and fix them is crucial to your development as an artist. You will not always have peers, a forum, or an instructor around to give input nor do you always want to rely on others for feedback. Comparing your work to others and being able to acknowledge your work's weaknesses doesn't make you a bad artist; in fact it makes you a better artist. The ability to see past the time and effort you've put into your own work and identify its shortcomings is an important trait of any production artist. The end user or viewer will not be able to appreciate how many hours you've spent or how many revisions you've done; all they see is the final image or result. Obviously a portfolio reviewer will be interested in the process, but only if the final product is good. Learn to look at your work honestly; this may mean comparing it with other's work or getting away from a piece for a little while and looking at it at a later time with fresh eyes.

Along with this ability to self-critique comes the ability to exercise self-control in regard to putting together a portfolio. This means resisting the urge to put every piece of art you've done since high school in your portfolio. When thinking about your portfolio it should be like comparing yourself to a musician's work; don't think of it as a complete back catalog of your art, but more like the greatest hits collection. Your portfolio should be able to be consumed rather quickly and leave a positive impression on the viewer. A portfolio shouldn't ask the viewer to trudge through a lot of your older, weaker pieces to find your most recent or best work. In fact, your most recent and hopefully best work should be the first thing in your portfolio. Pace your work out where your best work is upfront and another strong piece is at the end help to leave the viewer with a good impression. This assumes that there aren't too many average pieces in between. Remember to strike a balance of enough pieces that show your abilities but not so many that you water down your best work. I've seen portfolios that started off with a couple of really strong pieces that were followed up with what looked to be earlier, weaker work that ended up making it a middling portfolio. There is no perfect number of pieces to include; it's really about quality and variety.

Implementation of Your Work

It's important to have great-looking art in your portfolio, but as I mentioned in the previous chapters, half the job of 3d artists is technical problem solving. While it's not a requirement, it's worth attempting to get your work into a game engine if you haven't already. There are several reasons for this. First, you'll get to experience of a real workflow and this can in turn teach you a lot about how to build and set up your assets. This will also be one more bullet point on your resume: familiarity with a particular game engine. Lastly, it's a great place to take screenshots of your work. Modern engines have most of the bells and whistles found in traditional offline rendering packages; however, it is in real time and you can make revisions on the fly. There are a lot of high-quality engines worth checking out like Unreal and Unity, both of which are free to download and try.

While still images work for some disciplines like character art, environment art, and concepts, other disciplines like animation, visual effects, and even UI depend on video to show off their work. If you are putting a video in your portfolio, there are a couple of things to keep in mind. First off, avoid long intro sequences, long title shots and long black screen pauses; they can be very frustrating to sit through. Basically, avoid any "long" shots that aren't showing your actual work. Assume that the viewer doesn't have a lot of time and has a lot of other videos to review. It's best to get right into the content and really impress the viewer right off the bat. A proper soundtrack can enhance your visuals while a poor choice in music can really detract. Avoid cliché music or very loud music— pretty much anything that distracts from your work. Animations, visual effects, character spins, and even fly through shots of a level are ideal for the video format. Still shots of models, UV layouts or textures will not make the best use of video as a viewing format. As most video will receive some sort of compression even at high resolutions, still shots are best left to an image with little to no compression applied. You shouldn't feel the need to make a video if what you're showing can be better represented in still images.

Competition

Sometimes it's easy to look around and see your classmates as your only competition. In fact nothing could be further from the truth. Your classmates can become valuable contacts within the industry if they land a job before you. They know your work ethic, what you've done, and your personality. Also they will often know when a company is hiring before the postings are made public. For this reason, it's good to not look at your classmates as just competition but as possible future industry contacts.

In the past, when I've received an entry level candidate's portfolio and noticed that they went to the same school as another one of our team members, in these cases I'll always ask them for some feedback. Personal recommendations carry a lot of weight in games; who you know and how you conduct yourself is extremely important. This is a reality in the game industry in a large part due to how interconnected and small it really is. If you have worked in the industry for years and are applying at a new company, any previous coworkers that are at that company will most likely be asked about working with you. For this reason, it's important to remember one thing: don't be a jerk. I always take all personal feedback I solicited with a grain of salt, but it can help to paint a better picture of an applicant, especially because a resume and phone screen don't often tell the complete story.

In regard to your true competition, it's everyone else out there in schools and making games! Now that's a lot more overwhelming than just your classmates. To truly see what other artists are doing out there and what the competitive landscape looks like, it's a good idea to check out some popular art sites like Zbrush Central, ArtStation, and Polycount. Often when a game is finished, the artists will get their work together and do an "art dump" on the forums of these sites. If you're interested in seeing behind the curtain of art development on a major game, these are often your best chance. This can be extremely overwhelming when comparing yourself to this level of professional work. However, remember they were once starting out as well, everyone was. Also, keep in mind that anything you see from a game has been refined through rounds and rounds of feedback and sharing of knowledge from a lot of experienced individuals on the team.

Interview

Are There Any Skills besides the Ones Directly Related to the Position That You Look for?

Patrick Ingoldsby: Absolutely, I appreciate game artists that have a strong traditional background because they already have a well-practiced understanding of the artistic fundamentals that can make a compelling picture. Also it's easier to communicate "visually" with somebody on the team when you can both draw well on the whiteboard.

    I've also found that a lot of strong artists often have other creative interests they practice. Take an artist that is good at photography for example. They know how to objectively look for compositions in their world that can be framed and presented in a way that's visually striking. Very often the strongest character modelers also sculpt outside a computer. Having other creative interests outside making game art have transferrable traits that can strengthen your approach and quality in your contributions.

Keith Self-Ballard: I always try to get a read on the applicant's communication skills. Can they explain the artistic choices they make? Can they talk about their process? These types of questions provide insight into how well the person will be able to collaborate with others. The irony of traditional schooling is that it requires students to make a lot of choices for themselves. Development requires people to solve problems as a team. As such, they need to be able to explain their ideas and work through conflicting opinions. To be clear, this goes for both verbal communication and written. If I see an incoherent cover letter, that is a warning flag for me.

What, if Anything, Would You Like to See More of in a Portfolio?

Patrick: Strong portfolios tend to deliver not only the intimate isolated renders of assets but also how they sit in the world they're built for. Seeing both formats is a good way to communicate your understanding of world direction and your efforts made that visually make it believable.

Also, try to pick a couple of key assets for showcasing screenshots of your pipeline. You'd be surprised how much art directors appreciate samples of "behind the scenes" steps that were made in pieces development.

Keith: Self-critique. There are still a lot of portfolios out there that have way too many samples in them. My consistent feedback is that each and every piece must say something specific about your skills. The trouble with overloading your portfolio with lots of "stuff" is that you are more likely to include pieces that are weak.

    Employers grow concerned when they see weak content displayed in a portfolio next to strong content. Does the candidate not know the difference? How much did this person create themselves? Was their best piece a team project and someone else created the best aspects? So, when I say that I want to see more "self-critique," I mean that I want candidates to really reduce the volume of work to "the best" and cull the rest.

Conclusion

As we have seen, these are some of the important ideas to keep in mind when preparing a portfolio. It's not just the content; it's how you organize it as well as present it because at the end of the day, it's really how you are presenting yourself. In the following chapters we'll be looking at portfolio content and concepts for specific game art fields. We'll also delve into why the content is important and how you can demonstrate your competency in the field. We'll also be interviewing more industry professionals to get their take on the specifics of preparing a portfolio for their respective disciplines.

11

Crafting an Animation Portfolio

How you show your work is extremely important as an animator. Unlike other art disciplines that can be summed up in still images, an animation portfolio obviously needs to show off motion. This will usually come in the form of videos; however, there are browser-based 3d viewers available as well. Requiring anyone to download plugins is usually a terrible idea for a portfolio. However, it's a little more accepted and even likely that someone viewing an animation portfolio will already have the common animation-related plugins installed. When it comes to the actual videos and their format, this means don't pick an obscure video player or compression format; stick with the most common ones. The video needs good framing allowing the viewer to really see the complete action of the character or object. Often portfolio videos will play an animation a couple of times before cutting to the next animation. This is good because it allows the viewer to really take in the movement but also in the cases of a cycling animation it lets them see how well the animation loops. The reviewer will often be looking for things like good timing and weight to the movement but also at places where the cycle may not work or feel too repetitive.

While not a replacement for a well put together animation video reel, including a 3d viewer as previously mentioned is a good idea. The reason this isn't a catch-all replacement is because some people will not download any plugins either because of corporate policy or personal preference. You don't want to rely implicitly upon 3d viewers that require a plug-in download exclusively for all the content in your portfolio. When choosing one, it's important that it is capable of playing animation but also that it's not compressing your animation data in an undesirable way. One of the most universal 3d web viewers for game developers is the Unity viewer, as it is a pretty solid and recognized viewer. The advantage of a 3d viewer is that the portfolio reviewer will be able to rotate the model freely around allowing them to better judge the final animations. This can allow them a more in-depth look at your work, much more than a prerendered movie can. However, it's important to keep in mind that it makes it a lot easier to find the flaws in your work as well. Also, as of writing, the unity viewer does not work with the most recent version of Chrome. This change shows why it's a good idea to offer a basic way such as a common video format on your site as an alternative.

Interview

What Makes for a Solid Animation Portfolio?

Steve Madureira: Things that are relevant to the studio you are applying to. At Vigil, we were most interested in seeing walk/run cycles, idles, attacks, and things relevant to what we were doing. Seeing bipeds and quadrupeds is also good to see a wider variety of character types. We didn't care about lip-synching as much since that wasn't as big a part of our game (you can still definitely see good animation in acting though so if you have something good, be sure to put it in). If you are applying to a studio that works on children's games, you probably don't want to have a violent fatality animation in there, for example. Put your best things upfront and finish with something strong also. Don't fill the reel with fluff just to make it longer. If you have an animation you don't like very much, take it out. Only show your best work.

Leisel Madureira: A shorter portfolio is better than a super long one. Don't put anything in it that you aren't proud of just to flesh it out. If all you have left is a walk cycle and one attack for your reel, animate more, animate something you wouldn't be embarrassed to show your instructors or to future employers. Loud and obnoxious music is off putting in a portfolio; you don't want it to distract the viewer from the content. Instead of a video of animations strung together, some people link websites instead that have animations displayed individually. This makes viewing animations and replaying them easy for potential employers.

Chris Mead: First and foremost, every animation sample in a reel should be excellent. A single sub-par or unpolished animation can ruin the entire presentation. A solid animation reel should also have variety. A series of walk cycles and a few actions is not enough. The animator should demonstrate his ability to animate a diverse variety of characters, creatures, and machines. Animation samples should consist of a combination of individual game assets, multicharacter interactions, and cinematics. It's also very important to show the ability to animate in the style that the studio you are applying to is looking for.

The best reels show a variety of styles from traditional to realistic.

What Are Some Key Items That Are Must-Haves in a Portfolio for an Animation Position?

Leisel: You'll want your basic walk and run cycles. Attacks are a must. Having both bipedal and four-legged animals and creatures will help show you can tackle complex character movement. Also keep in mind who you're applying to. If you're applying to a studio that does mostly realistic war games, cartoony dog animations with a lot of squash and stretch won't illustrate as well what you can do for them as an animator, as a run and ledge grab, and gun and gun reloading animations would. You don't need to remove them completely, you never know what secret project they might be hiring for, but if they have a long history of action, first person shooter, or kids games, you might want to tailor your portfolio to reflect that. Be consistent, polished, and solid. Nothing is more confusing than seeing a mediocre animation in the middle of a solid demo reel. Don't make it overly long, or too short. Ask your instructors and peers for critique.

Movies versus Game Animations

Animation portfolios between movies and games can vary quite dramatically. Often in movies, there is a lead animator for a character and if it is a major character, there is often a sizeable team of animators dedicated to supporting that character. In games it's quite different; however, it can vary from company to company. At some companies an animator may move between different characters or be given several characters to focus on during the course of the project.

While a portfolio for movies is focused on showing personality and character emotion, a portfolio for games is concerned with this as well but with more emphasis on cycles and core movements. Cycles are animations that repeat like walk cycles, run cycles, etc. In video game animation portfolios it's important to show that you understand game animations. What does that mean? Take for example, in an animated movie a character might have to climb up on a box once in the entire film. An animator can really have a lot of fun making this a unique animation for the character. It can tell the personality of character; maybe for a clumsy character they struggle, loss their grip, and recover and then once they make it to the top they have a moment of relief. In a game the player may climb a box 500 times in the course of the game. While the movie animation approach may work the first time, the player will grow tired of the same animation over and over again, especially if it takes a few seconds each time. The key in almost all situations of game animations is to find the sweet spot of an animation that shows off the character's personality; however, it doesn't feel so predictable and repetitive that it grows stale. Also, most game animations need to be quick and feel responsive. If a player presses a button, there can't be a long slow wind up to see the action they intended to perform with their button press. What this means is if a player presses the jump button, within a few milliseconds not seconds, the player character needs to jump. Otherwise, the game controls will feel unresponsive and sluggish.

Cycles

Unless you are applying exclusively for a game cinematic animator position, cycles are going to be a very important part of your portfolio. Cycles or looping animations are the core element to game animator portfolio as there are often a lot of them in a game. Typical cycles include, but are not limited to, running, walking, sneaking, crouching walks, strafing left and right, backpedaling, and idling (see Figure 11.1). These are some of the most common things characters will do in most 3d games regardless of the genre. What a portfolio reviewer is looking for in the cycles is a good sense of motion, timing, weight, and obviously that the animation loops well.

The key to a good looping animation is that the viewer can't see where the loop ends or begins. Also, that there is nothing too unique about the animation that

Figure 11.1

Example of a run while holding a pistol looping cycle. Animation by Scott Marshall. (Used with the permission of Gunfire Games.)

11. Crafting an Animation Portfolio

shows the loop or breaks the illusion that the character is moving. For example in a run animation, if the character twists their torso to the left every time their left foot hits the ground but not the right, it becomes very obvious. Usually the goal of the locomotion cycles of a character is to give them enough personality that they are readable at distance and up close but not so much that it looks like there is something wrong with them. This doesn't mean you can't do "injured" walks or run animations; those should just be clear if that's what they are intended to be.

A slightly more complex animation set to show off would be an animation that has a nonlooping intro and ending that are tied together by a looping animation. An example of this would a charging forward animation. There would be a charge start where the character begins their run, a charge end where the character is coming out of the charge state, and the charging loop that would bridge the two. The reason behind this is often the distance a character will charge in game is never the same. Especially if it is a nonplayer character, their distance from the player or their intended target will always be different depending on the encounter.

Idles and Fidgets

Idle animations are required for almost every character because there is likely a point in the game where they are stationary. Idles in general need to be subtle and looping because any movements that are too dramatic or obvious will repeat very frequently resulting in an odd-looking character. Idles need to have little movement involved because almost every other animation for that character needs to be able to blend into it. This means an idle animation alone would be painfully boring to see a character do in a game for an extended period of time. To get around this, most characters have what are called fidget animations (see Figure 11.2). These are exactly what they sound like: they are small, isolated animations that introduce unique movement in the idle characters. Some common fidgets are look around, check hand or watch, check weapon, shrug shoulder stretch, shift weight, and shuffle feet. These will usually blend straight in from idle and give the character more personality. The key to any fidget animation is that it can seamlessly weave into the idle state and backout to it when the fidget is complete. Often these animations will be set to be random, both from an order they are played and time interval that they occur standpoint.

In addition to simple idle and fidgets, some games will introduce contextual sets of both. These can occur after an event or a specific sequence. For example, if a character just finished an intense sequence of running, the normal idle might be replaced with the character standing hunched over with their hands on their knees. Another example would be if the character is injured, the idle could represent with holding his/her side in pain. In addition to a unique idle, any fidgets would be relative to that new stance. These can help the character feel more alive and believable if they are reacting to the game world and its events around them.

Figure 11.2

War from *Darksiders*. The initial frame is his idle pose, while his fidgets include looking at his glove, looking his left, looking to his right, shrugging his shoulders, and shifting his weight. (Used with the permission of Nordic Games.)

Core Animations

Depending on the type of game or intent of the portfolio, there are a lot of animations outside of the looping ones that make up a character. Below are some examples to think about when starting an animation set for a character and the type of animations that might be used for that particular type of animation. These are the basics and can be extrapolated upon by doing more specific directional based or alternate versions. For example if you are doing a melee attack animation, you could just do a forward one. However, a full suite for a melee attack in a game may include an upward and downward strike. This level of variety could be extrapolated to any animations a character is doing.

For a melee-based character, some core animations would be, but not limited to, a couple of attacks, a combo chain with a finisher, getting hit from the front, back, left, and right, a jump, a death, a knockback, a recovery, a taunt, a parry, a stagger, a dodge, and a block. Of course this list can grow to include more specific things depending on your character like shield bashes, enrages, counters, and whatever else you want to add. For a caster-based character in a fantasy game, some of the core animations could be very similar to the melee character with the addition of a charge up animation, an area of effect blast animation, a channeling animation, and a couple of casting animations.

For a more realistic game focused on firearms, often animations are classified into types of guns as the animations and the poses can change dramatically between say a pistol and a rifle. It may be easier to think about these animations as gun-specific actions with modifiers. For example if you want to make a suite of walking animations for a character carrying a pistol, you'd want to include walking while drawing the weapon, walking while aiming, walking while shooting, walking while reloading, and strafe walking while aiming. For crouching it would be very similar: crouching while drawing a weapon, aiming, shooting, reloading, and standing to crouching and standing up from the crouch. This same list of animations could then be applied to a character holding a rifle.

One thing to keep in mind is that most modern game engines use blend or additive animation systems. What this means is animators will often create animations in a compartmentalized way. For example, an animator will create a walk cycle and aim animation separately; then in the game engine the two will be combined to either be blended or added together meaning the lower portion of the walk will not be modified but the aim is layered on top and overrides the previous upper body portion of the walk. It is an option for an animator who is a little more tech savvy or up for a challenge to set up some animations in their portfolio like this. This shows initiative at learning how a lot of animation is set up in some games. This responsibility can often fall on technical animators or designers depending on the company.

Character Interactions

Another important type of animation for characters in games is interactions. The player character will often interact with quite a few different inanimate objects as well as other characters throughout the course of a game; so it's a good idea to include some of these in your portfolio. When approaching what interactions you have the character do, it's not a bad idea to keep them consistent with the animation theme you have done so far as well as the character's theme. This means not having a barbarian interacting with a computer keyboard, though that may yield some humorous results. These animations will usually be a singular animation set that would be triggered by a button press by the player. For a typical modern shooter this could include, typing on a keyboard, opening a door, pressing a button, or forcing an elevator door open. Some of these animations, like forcing a door open, are a great opportunity to show off your understanding of the core principles of animation like staging, anticipation and follow through as well as demonstrating a good sense of weight.

Another type of interaction is that of the character with other characters. This could encompass a lot of different animations from rescuing an injured character to grappling over a weapon to stealth attacking another character. While companies and game engines all have different ways of actually making two characters interact in game through programming and animation systems, showing you have a fundamental understanding of how two characters interact from an animator perspective is what's really important. These animations can often be more complex and may take longer than some of the previously mentioned isolated animations, however, they are great at showing the depth of an animator's skill set.

Motion Capture

Motion Capture or Mo-cap, as it is predominately known, is the capturing of motion data by way of recording the movement of actors through the use of special cameras and equipment. A hard reality for animators is that a lot of studios rely upon motion capture data for most of their animations. Mo-cap, like any other process, is not free of flaws. Often animators will need to comb through the motion capture files and clean them up, looking for any bad data, or captured movement that just didn't translate well visually. In these cases, the animators will still be able to utilize their animation skills; however, it may be in a much more limited capacity than a game that all the animation is done from scratch.

The other hard reality for those looking to get into games is that studios that do motion capture-based animations look for motion capture experience in an animator position. Unfortunately this is one of the hardest skills to come by unless your school has motion capture data on hand or you find some data posted online. Assuming neither of these are options for you, the best thing you can do as an animator is to refine your skills and learn the tools available to you. This means become very familiar with how the 3d program you work in handles lots of per frame data and learn the tools you need to use to work with it. Much like any animation position, having solid animation skills will help as well.

Interview

What Makes One Portfolio Stick Out More Than Others?

Steve Madureira: Strong, consistent animation.

Leisel Madureira: Keep your characters and environments simple so that your animation is the main focus. Acting animations with dialog are fine, and can show you can express emotion and pay attention to detail, but that is more appropriate for applying to animation studios in the television and movie industries. If you can animate personality into an action, like a walk, a run, a climb, a jump, that will help your reel stand out more. That's not to say you need to make it cartoony, but adding character and personality to a walk to express confidence, arrogance, nervousness, that'll help show you can do more than animate generic, "samey" walks and runs.

What Advice Can You Give for Those Working in a Professional Environment for the First Time?

Steve: Be sure you love animating or games (preferably both). Passion for what you're working on will show up in the quality of your work. Use reference as often as you can and ask for feedback often. Don't be offended by feedback and apply what you hear back from your lead. You will be redoing animations and tweaking them a lot. Make friends at work; you spend a long time there and you work closely with them a lot.

Leisel: Ask for feedback and be receptive to it. With their experience, they'll have a better eye for animation than you do fresh out of school. Communicate with people and learn as much as you can from your coworkers, and learn even more on your own by looking up solutions on the Internet, and exploring assets in your game. Your coworkers are a valuable resource, but also understand they have their own work to get done. Make friends with your office mates. You will be sitting with them all day in and out. You want to, at the very least, not find each other unpleasant, especially if there's any crunching to be done down the road. If you're lucky you'll make lasting friendships. Chances are, no matter where you end up, you will work with old coworkers again at another studio. It's a small industry.

Conclusion

A good animation portfolio hits on all the points we went over in this chapter and delivers on them. The core of any animation portfolio is variety and showing your versatility as an animator. This means variety in characters, variety in styles, and variety in types of animations. Also, it's important to avoid including weaker animations in an attempt to fill out your portfolio. It's better to only show your best and have a shorter reel than including pieces that pull your entire presentation down. Animation in games is a highly competitive field and there are a lot of animators out there.

12

Crafting a Character Art Portfolio

When applying for a character art position, it's important to consider a couple of things. The first is this hard truth; there are a lot more people who want to be character artists versus actual positions available. What this means is usually you have to be very skilled at being a character artist to find a job. One of the reasons for this disparity in applicants and open positions is that character work is thought of as prestigious. After all you are making the characters in the game. The other reason is that character artists are very specialized and they usually work on characters throughout the entire project until there are no more characters left. Much like concept artists, toward the last cycles of a game's development when the characters are finished there won't be a lot for the character artists to do other than some minor optimizations and possibly work for expansions or downloadable content. Lastly, most games have a limited number of characters. What this means is while a project may have 10 environment artists they may only have need for 3 character artists. This isn't a set ratio, but most of the time the character team will be smaller than most of the other art disciplines.

Knowing this, how do you get a job as a character artist? As mentioned previously in Chapter 4, the key skills a character artist must have are a great understanding of anatomy, color, shape, and texturing. In addition to this, having a great imagination and the ability to extrapolate from an idea plays heavy into the role as well. The detail of a piece of concept art a character artist may receive can vary greatly. In some cases, it may be a highly detailed front, side, and three-quarter view of a character while in other cases it may be a loose sketch of a character in a pose. It could be either of these, or anywhere in between; the key for a character artist is to take that concept and create a 3d model that looks like the concept while maintaining the given style on the game. The ability to produce a variety of styles is probably one of the most important skills you want to show off in your portfolio.

Interview

What Are Some Items That Are Must-Haves in a Portfolio for a Character Artist?

Brian "Bobo" Jones: Two key elements that should be in your portfolio would be a character that shows a strong understanding of anatomy and a "wow factor" character. A "wow factor" character would be a piece that people will associate with you as an artist. I often remember people not by their name but by their portfolio. This piece should be original if at all possible. If you have a hard time coming up with something original, commission or partner with a concept artist. You could do an amazing Superman but what makes your superman stand out from the other thousands of Superman's out there?

Adam Pitts: Attention to detail. The technology is getting so good, it's getting harder and harder to tell computer graphics (CG) from real life, and artists are expected to toe the line with that in mind. Pick an iconic celebrity, and try to match likeness to nearly 100%—if you can do that you will impress. If your character art is in line with a more stylized approach, have enough character examples to convey an idea about the style. Look at the character line up for *Team Fortress 2* as an example of what I mean—they belong in the same universe and are cohesive.

Tohan Kim: Strong understanding of anatomy, being able to convey facial expressions and emotions, and being able to work to a style guide.

Stylization

The goal of your portfolio should be to show variety and different approaches to characters because it may open up unique opportunities when applying to different companies. If your portfolio only has heavily stylized and colorful characters, a company making a game with more realistic characters will often pass it over. The opposite is true of having a portfolio focused on realism when being reviewed by a company doing stylized work. This may seem unfair and somewhat of a snap judgment, but a company wants to know if an applicant is capable of delivering what they are looking for. This is why variety is so important. You as an artist may be fully capable of producing other types of characters than what you have in your portfolio, but it begs the question, "Why isn't it in your portfolio?" A company reviewing your work really only knows what you are capable of by what you have in your portfolio. That's the reason that portfolio content, layout, and self-critique are so important to the creation of a portfolio.

Inclusion of many styles ranging from realistic to stylized examples of work is crucial to showing your abilities as a character artist; however, it is important to truly understand stylization. There is an old adage in art that one must understand the rules before they can truly break free of them. This is the case with stylization particularly in the application anatomy of a character. Skipping anatomy lessons to jump into stylization will almost always produce poor results. Even in one of the most revered examples of stylization in games, *Team Fortress 2*, the characters while highly exaggerated adhere to rules of anatomy.

Beyond anatomy stylization, texture and surfaces detail can be stylized as well (see Figure 12.1). This doesn't mean making very flat solid-colored textures under the guise of stylization. If anything, good stylization can actually be harder than doing pure realism. With the realism approach, you can compare real images

Figure 12.1

Lilith from *Darksiders II: Deathinitive Edition.* (Used with the permission of Nordic Games.)

and gather texture references and surface detail images. With stylization, you are simplifying all that and completely relying on the strength of the shapes, color, and silhouette to describe your character. Some people go for stylized characters because they think it's the easier approach; great character artists know it's actually more challenging.

History

History is such an important element of character art that it deserves its own section. This means the wear and tear found on character clothes, armor, weapons, or even the face and body (see Figure 12.2). Sometimes when making a character, people focus heavily on the ideal material state of an item and their final art can look a little too pristine and lifeless. It's important to layer on some history to any character. Whether it's a grizzled medieval knight with sword dings and scuffs on his armor from his countless battles to a modern day adventurer with threadbare jeans and worn leather belts and holster from all the parkour they've been doing.

There is an opposite approach which some artists will take, that is too much damage all over the place. Again, tell a story, but also think about how a character would receive their damage. The knight would not have equally distributed wear and dings all over their armor unless they were being drug behind a horse over gravel roads regularly. So assuming this is not the back story for your character, think about how and where the character's armor would receive wear. For example if we're talking about metal armor, thin outward-facing edges and trim edges would receive the most of the dings and dents as they are often the most exposed parts. The spots where the armor overlaps would see some wear from repetitive movement in the form of scratches and scuffs. Also the spots of overlap

Figure 12.2

Example of characters with history, Constructs from *Darksiders II: Deathinitive Edition*. The metal shows signs of combat as well as age. Models by Tohan Kim. (Used with the permission of Nordic Games.)

in addition to the deepest crevices would see the largest collection of dirt and oxidization. Small dents here and there can add some general history as long as it's not heavy handed. Lastly adding specific larger spots of damage can tell particular visual stories, like a larger dent across the chest plate can weave a story of the character narrowly escaping certain death. Creating a character and writing up a bio is a perfectly fine exercise; however, why tell when you can show the story? If you've created the medieval knight mentioned earlier, show his story through his clothing. Work in the dents and scuffs as opposed to adjectives.

Weapons

Depending on the game and the company, some companies employ artists that only focus on weapons, while other companies expect character artists to handle creating weapons. As a character artist starting out, it's a good idea to have at least a couple of weapon examples in your portfolio. This can range from realistic to fantasy to sci-fi, swords to guns to sword guns. Much like character design, weapon design has a heavy focus on a strong and interesting silhouette. In terms of fire arms, an understanding of how actual fire arms function in relation to reloading and the firing mechanisms helps a lot when creating 3d models of guns whether they are realistic or fantastical. This extra step of applying some believability to a weapon helps to ground the weapon in its world regardless of how fantastical of a world it is.

We briefly touched on "history" earlier but it's important to note that weapons need damage as well (see Figure 12.3). Whether its swords or guns, weapons should show some of the same elements of damage mentioned previously. There is a trend in games that even when the player has the option to purchase a brand new weapon, the weapon looks like it's seen a couple of tours of duty on the battlefield. This may seem a bit odd, because if you're purchasing a new gun in real life, you don't expect it to look scuffed and beat up. However, the reason for this in games is that it makes the weapons look more interesting. Clean guns in games often look very stark and even fake at times. Again it's that history that sells the realism and believability of an item. Adding edge wear and some surface wear can make gun or sword much more visually interesting.

Attention to Detail Exercise

In this exercise, we'll be looking at an antique pistol and some of its unique detail. It's important to note how guns actually show age and wear and take that knowledge into consideration when you make a gun in 3d. Proper application of damage can help to sell the believability of the weapon.

A. The first thing to note is the consistent wear on the beveled edge. This occurs because it's one of the few "hard" edges on surface of the gun

Figure 12.3

A detailed image of a worn flintlock pistol. A–C looks at some of the specific details that sell it's wear and tear. (Copyright iStock.com/Jason Lugo. With permission.)

and also where the most interaction with the gun occurs. This edge will come in contact with more surfaces than any other part of the gun, so the polish will wear off the quickest in these locations, exposing the underlying raw wood.

B. The next thing to notice is the difference in the wood on the grip and the barrel. The level of shine as well as damage is quite noticeably different. This is because during use the grip comes in contact with a person's hand far more frequently than the barrel does. The natural oils from a person's hand keeps the grip oiled and thus more protected than the barrel. The chips seen on the barrel are likely due to the protective oil or seal wearing off and leaving the wood unprotected and more susceptible to damage.

C. It's important to note that while this gun is an antique, it has been up kept and is likely in working condition. This is probably why you don't notice any rust present on the metal. The metal is old and has a lot of surface detail and character, but no rust. It is worth noting that dust and "crud" is collected around the nonmoving parts of the hammer and pan. This detail adds to the age and authenticity of a gun.

Much like with armor and clothing you can go too far. Adding too much dirt or rust can make the weapon unbelievable very quickly. First off, rusty guns are frequently used in games as a mechanism to signify the weapons' unreliability as well as telling the player it's not an ideal weapon choice. Also, rust on things in games, in particular on weapons, can get very busy. Unless a gun is sitting in a swamp for years on end, the rust isn't going to be equally distributed across the model. Most guns are manufactured not to rust, because real rusty guns are very unreliable. That isn't to say guns don't rust; however, when they do, much like any metal, they start in areas where the metal is close and overlapping. This is because moisture can get caught in these spaces making it an ideal location for oxidization to occur. Keep these things in mind when adding age to weapons.

Interview

Are There Any Skills besides the Ones Directly Related to the Position You Look for?

Brian "Bobo" Jones: Social skills go a long way. You are a member of a team and need to be able to communicate and generally "fit in" with the others. Remember that this industry is fairly close knit. There are some artists out there that are great talents but have a reputation for being hard to work with. This can hinder their chances of employment and/or advancement.

Adam Pitts: Personally, I look for someone with an eye for composition. The ability to balance visual elements is a skill important for any artist, and is the one that I see most young guys don't have developed. Most of the younger artists focus too much on the individual components of what they are working on (which is fine in terms of quality) but neglect how the asset looks and works when all its parts come together as a whole.

What Are the Most Common Mistakes You See in a Portfolio?

Brian: The most common mistake I see in a portfolio of an artist trying to get into the industry is too much content. I would much rather see four or five very strong pieces than 20 mediocre ones. I recommend having a "portfolio" section and a "sketch/blog" section. Portfolio section should just be your best highly polished pieces. Sketch section should have your other work that isn't finished or as polished. This way I know you have the ability to bring anything to completion but I can also see some of your thought process, construction, and creativity in your loser work. Of course once you have industry experience, your portfolio will grow with professional pieces.

Adam: A weak piece. If something is not your best, don't include it. Don't judge this yourself either; as artists we are often biased to own art. Ask a peer or someone already in the industry what they think, and don't be offended if they are honest with you!

Tohan: Someone would include everything in his portfolio since he loves all of his work so much. You need to consider including only a few pieces that you and others think are your best. You need to highlight your strength rather than showing your mistakes.

What, if Anything, Would You Like to See More of in a Character Portfolio?

Brian: An ideal portfolio would have an anatomy study, fantasy piece, and a sci-fi piece. Among these, it would be nice to see both male and females explored as well as examples of realistic and stylized proportions. The anatomy piece should be of a realistic human. The fantasy piece can show off the heroic over the top proportions we associate with comics and games and the sci-fi piece should show an understanding of hard surface modeling.

Adam: As mentioned before, I'm a sucker for composition and balance within art. It's that quality that when you look at something you might not know immediately why you like it, but it just feels right. Presentation goes a long way also; show your models with nice lighting and a good render. At the very least it shows you have an artistic eye. Wireframes and UV layouts are nice to see, but honestly that's easy to teach someone because it's just a technical skill; the harder part is having the eye for good art in the first place.

Tohan: I would like to see concept and final character art work together so that I could see how well this person understands the concept. Even if this person has a problem with concept, it would give us a chance to see whether this person can transcend his creativity.

Personality

Every good character in any form of entertainment has personality. This is communicated through not only how they act and carry themselves, but how they look and what they wear. This is no different in games. Your portfolio is the time to show off all the skills we've looked at in Chapter 4 and apply those to creating a "character" with personality (see Figure 12.4). There is no better way to show the complexities and depth of your own personality than through artistic expression.

Figure 12.4

Straga from *Darksiders*. Model by Brian "Bobo" Jones. (Used with the permission of Nordic Games.)

12. Crafting a Character Art Portfolio

Which begs the questions, why make a bland lifeless character? Characters take time to make, so spend that time making a character that is full of visual interest and personality. Make something unique that says "you." Having interesting characters in your portfolio will make your portfolio more memorable to viewers. This is especially important when your portfolio is likely one of hundreds a company may receive for a single position. Anything you can do to make the reviewers take note and remember your work is important. Also, it's worth noting that this available position to applicant range is actually quiet realistic when it comes to any game art position, but is especially true in regard to character art positions. Knowing the odds, why would you waste time making a boring character?

Adaptability

One of the toughest things a character artist needs to learn early on is the skill of adaptability. This comes in two forms: style and technical. First let's look at style adaptability. Characters have some of the greatest potential for subtle variance due to both proportions and shape treatment. Many character artists looking to get into games will have developed their own style and approach for characters as they've learned how to sculpt and texture. This can be a problem if you are not able to easily adapt your style to match someone else's. The goal of any game is for all the characters to look similar, as if they belong in the same world. This is primarily achieved by adhering to specific proportions, shape treatment, and texturing. Often in development, a style will be established early on and the character artists are expected to follow suite on all the characters from that point forward. This can be somewhat challenging when first starting out because you may only know one approach to crafting a character. This is where, when crafting a portfolio, variety in your content is so important. Having examples of different takes on styles and looks can show that you are fully capable of emulating other styles and looks.

The second part of this concept of adaptability is more of a technical skill. Having a singular way of making characters and not easily diverging from that can be a hindrance. Character pipelines are dictated by what the characters do in the game. There are some games where the characters never change throughout the course of the game. This means the pipeline to creating them might not be very difficult and is likely very straightforward. However, a game where the characters are able to change their outfits, hair, color of outfit, or hair style will require a much more complex art creation pipeline. As a character artist, it's important to be ready for anything. The example of very straightforward character pipelines has nothing that needs to be illustrated in a portfolio other than showing quality characters. When it comes to accounting for a more complex system, one thing you can do to represent this in your portfolio is to approach a character model in a modular fashion. A good way to do this is to generate another interchangeable outfit for the character, a different hair style, or a completely unique color variant.

User-Generated Content

In recent years a new outlet has opened up for 3d artists interested in contributing to an existing game and making money in the process. Valve has led the charge on this front, allowing users to create content and charge for it in two of their biggest games: *Dota* and *Team Fortress 2*. Through the steam workshop, users can generate assets for existing characters and sell it on the game's marketplace. Additionally, Unreal allows users to generate and sell content for the *Unreal 4* game engine as well for their *Unreal Tournament* game currently in development. Due to the popularity and accessibility of these games, this can actually be a way to make money on a game without working at a company. While the potential to make money is quite alluring it's also a great opportunity to create content that is ideal for your portfolio. Creating assets for these games is just like in any other game. There are asset budgets you must adhere to and technical specifications you must follow. These pieces show well in your portfolio because they serve as an example of experience. While it's not on a team, it is the experience of working on a live game with real assets.

Beyond these options that allow you the chance to make money, there are a lot of other games that allow the user to add content. Some can be very robust with the tools provided to them and let the user modify a lot, while others may only allow the user to replace UI or textures. Modding a game by adding your own characters into it can be quite a valuable experience. It gives you the opportunity to learn and utilize a company's pipeline to get your art into a game. Some of these may be very poorly implemented and lack proper documentation but some can be very easy to use. Again, this is a good opportunity to get some real-world game development experience under your belt as well as unique content in your portfolio.

Conclusion

We've looked at the skills it takes to be a character artist as well as ways to approach your work to help it stick out from other portfolios. Character art is a highly competitive field and there are a lot of amazing character artists out there, but don't get discouraged. As with any art, the more you do something, the better you get at it. The same is true of characters, during the process of creating a character you will often find things to improve upon in your next character. Keep those things in mind when moving forward and always work to refine those core character art skillsets. In the end, a solid character art portfolio boils down to a great understanding of anatomy, application of color theory, attention to detail, and selling a character's personality.

13

Crafting a Concept Art Portfolio

As mentioned in Chapter 5, concept art isn't just the ability to draw or even draw well. It's really about invention and follow-through on that invention. When it comes to preparing a portfolio, it's not just important to have good-looking work but much like math it's important to show how you arrived at your final answer. This means showing the thumbnails, and showing the roughs that came before the final piece. This is especially important for someone trying to break into the industry as they won't usually have a large variety of work from shipped games. Someone without prior experience really needs to prove they understand the job. The best way to do this is to show the steps along the way that got you to your final product. It gives the reviewer a chance to see your thought process as an artist, and that you are able to make critical decisions. As a concept artist, this comes into play every time you create a handful of thumbnails and choose one to take to the next step.

Often concept artist will have a preferred type of concept they like to do; this often falls along the lines of characters or environments. There is nothing wrong with enjoying or focusing on one or the other and oftentimes the skillsets can be very different depending on the scope of the game. It is, however, good to be able to hop the concept fence and work on the other side if needed. This will make you a more versatile artist thus making you more valuable.

Interview

What Makes for a Solid Concept Art Portfolio?

Ryan Gitter: Good design.

Seriously that's really it; when I review portfolios the thing guaranteed to get my support is strong design skills. Storytelling ability is second and also very important. Technical abilities like painting skills or drawing abilities are definitely a necessity, but they are secondary to the first things I listed.

Christopher J. Anderson: Be well rounded. Show various types of concept art such as environments, characters, etc. Show several at a high level of polish, and a few at earlier stages of development. Sometimes a portfolio can be very specific such as very character driven, which will land a character concept job. Those characters should be very diverse in subject matter, allowing the artist to be well rounded within that area.

Having a solid portfolio is determined on the skill level of the artist; for instance, is this person a senior, or a junior? Juniors just need to show they can do a decent job. Seniors need to show that they are very experienced, they are a master at their craft, and can guide the juniors who may not be masters yet, but have great potential.

What makes a solid portfolio is also determined by what type of concept artist you are. For example if you're a "category" concept artist, then make sure your character portfolio for instance is highly competitive. If you're going for the position of working on a *zombie* game, your character concept art portfolio should have enough diversity in themes that you should have examples of characters that you can match the needs. If you have a full concept portfolio, your portfolio should be diverse enough to show that you can do several themes for each category such as environments, characters, etc.

What Are the Most Common Mistakes You See in a Portfolio?

Chris: There are many. One is abstract art being presented as concept art. This is when a portfolio is filled with environment concepts, for instance, that are too abstract to fully understand what is being seen. A few of these are fine; however, if most of the portfolio consists of this, 3d artists will have a difficult time building from the concepts. This will snowball into bigger problems down the road.

Style

Although this may seem counter-intuitive, having a particular style to your work can sometimes be a determinant as much as it can work in your favor. As an illustrator or comic book artist it's important to have your own style that makes your work stand out from others. This is not really the case with concept art. Everyone's work has a style to some degree; it's really a representation of every artist you've enjoyed or learned from in the past. However, having a portfolio that is entirely in one particular style can act as a blocker for getting a job. This is especially true if the reviewer is looking for a general concept artist they may click past you portfolio after giving it only a quick glance.

As an artist, particularly a concept artist, on some level you want to have an identity and a signature style; however, it's good to do a couple of pieces that are outside of this comfort zone. In the end, this makes you a more well-rounded artist and a more desirable candidate as well. This isn't completely necessary, as you can stick to a style you are comfortable with, but it's important to remember in doing that it may severely limit potential opportunities.

Style isn't just how you craft your work; it's how you approach the proportions to your work, the way you apply color, the way you approach big and small shapes. Starting out, it's a great idea to try different styles out to see what fits your work flow the best. As an artist your style will grow and mature with every piece you do; so it's a great idea to keep drawing, always.

Subject Matter

The other habit concept artists can fall into that's detrimental to their job search is sticking to a singular subject matter. Just like with style, this can be a very negative thing if your chosen subject matter isn't in line directly with the company you're applying to. This can mean a heavy focus on a particular genre or even a focus on a singular type of character. Being a concept artist means you are a visual inventor; however, if your portfolio has a bunch of work that all looks identical, you lose credibility as a person who is inventive and versatile.

Most games require a lot of different approaches to art designs, different themes, and visual cues to help differentiate the different parts of the game. A game with a singular look to the world and similar characters can come across very boring and flat after a while. When approaching concepts for your portfolio and you find yourself struggling to come up with new ideas, pick some completely different games or genres as a starting point and try to find ways to expand on those ideas, or take them in a completely new direction. All great art is built upon the foundation of the previous art that came before it.

Invention

As mentioned early, a concept artist is a visual problem solver. This is accomplished through creative invention. While it's important to understand both the visual history of art and the modern trends in games, it's important to be able to build upon that knowledge and create something special. With so many creative mediums out there, movies, comics, games, etc., pure invention is nearly

Figure 13.1

Example of robot companions for a sci-fi game. Concepts by Dan Beaulieu. (Used with the permission of Gunfire Games.)

impossible. However, that isn't any reason to lose hope. Creating your own take on something and making it your own is really what will make your portfolio standout from other applicants. Take a robot for example; there have been thousands of designs for robots over the years. However, every so often someone does a new unique take on them (see Figure 13.1). Breaking the conventions of an idea and making it something distinctive is memorable, as opposed to following the trends that have been previously set forth.

Anatomy

To be a concept artist, a fantastic grasp of anatomy is a must, in particular human proportions and the underlying bone and muscle structure. Sometimes artists think they can neglect this skill or completely ignore it, possibly because they assume they'll just draw clothing on top of it or because they want to focus on stylized proportions. These aren't valid reasons to skip the anatomy lessons; in fact they really reinforce the importance of an understanding of anatomy. To draw outfits, armor, or characters in general, the importance of the underlying structure cannot be overstated. Understanding the underlying anatomy means the armor or outfit will adhere to body correctly and will structurally be able to be built and animated in 3d. It is possible to make a great-looking picture that can't actually be translated into a 3d model due to inaccuracies in the proportions and anatomy or even the "Escher effect." This can occur when an artist doesn't consider the feasibility of what they are drawing or how something actually would work in 3d.

Strong skills in anatomy and physique means as a concept artist, the human form won't be the time-consuming part of your concept; the conceptualization will be. Not having to think about the character's anatomy means it comes as second nature, and your design will be strong and also able to be modeled on a human character (see Figure 13.2). This isn't to say you can't use life reference when starting a concept; it just means you can move quickly through the initial proportion steps and dig into the meat of your design.

Figure 13.2

Example of a character design taken from thumbnails to final concept while being conscience of the character's anatomy. Concept by Christopher J. Anderson.

Additionally, correct anatomy is more visually pleasing and actually can act as a better delivery method for your ideas. This may sound insane, but is very much the case. If you take the same design and put it on an anatomically correct drawing and a nonanatomically correct drawing (regardless of proportion stylizations), the anatomical one will always be picked. The nonanatomical one will most likely receive critiques on the design that the correct one has as well. This is due to the "uncanny valley" concept. People are more accepting of things that match up with anatomical knowledge we all have for human beings. That's why the best humanoid monster designs will often have altered human proportions. This is because our brain recognizes that as wrong and therefore feels uncomfortable on some level when viewing it. This is not the feeling you want to give someone when they are viewing what is supposed to be a "normal" human design.

Lastly, figure drawings aren't required in a concept artist's portfolio, but if you have good figure drawings, include them. By the same token, if it's not good, omit it. Bad figure drawings do more damage to a portfolio than good drawing can do to improve it. When it comes to good figure drawing, the level of detail and rendering isn't what's important; it really comes down to nailing shape and proportions of the models and conveying that in the piece. The line work should be confident but can remain very loose if it describes the form accurately.

Environments

Often the focus of environmental concept is to establish look, shape, color, mood, and lighting (see Figure 13.3). The focus isn't often detail. It can be but that is very time-consuming. Detail is usually saved for what is aptly named "call outs." These call outs can be props that are needed for the environment; they can be things that are implied or referenced in the larger environmental concept. Often environment concepts are approached as large swaths of color and texture; however, they can also be much more detailed line of work if structure and proportion details are required.

Attention to Detail Exercise

In this exercise we're going to look at a concept by Christopher J. Anderson. There is a lot of information packed into this image. It informs the viewer with a lot of details without any words.

A. *First is scale.* By placing a human figure in the doorway the viewer is instantly informed of the scale of this structure. Without the human for reference, the actual size of the tower could be debatable.

B. *Materials.* Through application of color and shape, the viewer can easily discern that the tower is made of a cobbled stone and the roof is made of thatch. To an outside viewer not familiar with the lore of these people are also informed of the level of technology of the people that

Figure 13.3

Example of a defensive tower. A–D focuses on some of the details that help to build a visual narrative. Concept by Christopher J. Anderson.

built it. The makeshift nature of the roof structure and the different shaped rocks that make up the tower are not only visually interesting but also telling the abilities of the original architects.

C. The archer serves some of the same purposes as the man in the doorway, to establish scale. Also the archer is aiming his bow, which tells the viewer that this is either a battlefield tower or a defensive position. Additionally, both humans being in armor reiterates that point.

D. Lastly, the tower is set in a world. There is not a lot of detail in the surrounding world but the grassy plains and rain ground that add a lot of context. The lighting gives a hint of a somber mood and adds an extra level of "texture" to the image that wouldn't have been present if it were sitting on a white backdrop.

Due to the sheer number of unique environments and locations needed to flesh out a game world, besides key art and early proof of concept pieces, most environmental concept art is focused on inspiring through mood, lighting, and structure (see Figure 13.4). Often the details are left loose; this is partially to allow the concept artist to provide a larger pool of concepts as opposed to only a few very detailed ones. Sometimes specific key areas or parts will be called out and the assumption is that the rest of the lesser areas can be derived from the specific areas.

Starting out as a concept artist, it's a great idea to not only show you final work but your roughs or thumbnails for a particular piece (see Figure 13.5). Again,

Figure 13.4

Example of a concept focused on the mood, lighting, and ambiance of an area as opposed to specific details. Concept by Ryan Gitter.

showing off you work flow gives the viewer a chance to see your thought process and visual problem-solving abilities. Seeing examples of your rough pencil work shows that you have strong traditional skills as well.

When it comes to environments in a concept portfolio, variety is the key. Concepts that span different themes, time periods, styles, and genres are all valid. Additionally, it's worth approaching the concepts with different goals. As we've looked at so far, concept artists have a variety of pre- and post-production duties. One of these duties as we've looked at is focusing on mood and color for an area of the game. The goals here are high-level look and feel as opposed to specifics.

As we've touched on, paint overs are quiet common in the full production of a game and are usually approached as quick pieces to help out a 3d artist by generating some ideas in an existing scene. In these cases a 3d artist may have done an initial art pass on a scene, but the scene still needs something "more." Often the concept artist will then be tasked with painting over the in-game screenshots of a scene (see Figure 13.6). The concept artist will usually be given constraints based on what's possible as well as limitations set forth by the game design. From there, a concept artist will paint directly over the screenshots adding or removing elements, introducing new colors and shapes, or even completely changing the visual flow. After this is finished and approved, the 3d artist will then attempt to mimic the ideas the concept artist has introduced. Sometimes a concept artist is brought in right after a designer finishes a layout but before the environment artists even touch it. This may be the hardest type of image to include in a concept portfolio because you will need a starting point. This can, however, be accomplished if you are familiar at all with a 3d program or even SketchUp. Using those programs you can build out a simple space and then paint over it.

Figure 13.5

This is example of a rough and color final key art piece from Super Fuse Ball by Dan Beaulieu. Seeing the rough sketch to final really shows off the attention to making the perspective work as well as the focus on shape language and character early on. (Image used with the permission of Gunfire Games.)

An example of paint over of a level laid out using modular pieces. Concept by Dan Beaulieu. (Used with the permission of Gunfire Games.)

Characters

As with any portfolio, character concepts are all about the variety. As I mentioned earlier, finding unique or different spins on previously visited ideas isn't a bad thing. At least it's better than an identical retread. So what should you think about when creating a character? Sometimes it's easy to get over excited and stack detail on top of detail in a character concept. This is often a bad idea unless the character is meant to be some sort of trinket collecting hermit. Realistically, good character design is clean, readable, and iconic (see Figure 13.7). Nathan Drake from *Uncharted*, Master Chief from *Halo*, Dante from *Devil May Cry* all have very readable designs. They're not overburdened with details or a lot of "stuff" all over them. This is because their designs are strong on their own. When designing

Figure 13.7

Character portrait concept by Christopher J. Anderson.

a character, the same ideas that go into 2d design should be applied: focus on color, shape, and size of those elements. Color is important because it identifies the character, both in isolation and when they are in their world.

When crafting a character concept at a game company, the final intention is usually for someone to build it in 3d. To provide the most useful concept, an artist should provide as much detail as possible. This usually includes callout to any particular elements that are key to the character's design (see Figure 13.8). This can take the form of a very detailed concept or even boxed out areas of a concept that the 3d artist should pay particular attention to. Additionally, many 3d artists like to have a turnaround of the character to fully understand the proportions and how the outfit works. This could include an orthographic front, side and rear or just a rear shot. The more information you provide in a concept the easier it is for the 3d artist to nail the ideas of the concept.

Lastly, try color studies. Once you've finished a piece try changing the colors you used on the character. Show a couple of the variants you've come up with. This doesn't mean just shifting the hue slider in Photoshop. Think about how color was used in the initial piece and then apply different colors in this same manner. This shows your knowledge of color application and color theory when it comes to

Figure 13.8

Example of a detailed character concept with turnarounds. Concept by Christopher J. Anderson.

character design. Also, many companies like to create color variants of characters in games as it gives a little more variety and is relatively easy to do on 3d models.

Weapons

While this could've been a subsection of characters, I feel like it deserves its own section because so many games have some sort of weapon in them. These weapons, unless based directly on real-world guns, need concepts. When it comes to unique gun designs, the intricacy of the asset comes down to the type of game and the perspective at which the world is viewed. First-person focused shooters need very high fidelity details and interesting, intricate designs because besides the character's hands, the gun is the only representation of the player in the moment-to-moment game play. This means they should be treated like characters. They need to be visually interesting and have some level of complexity to them that make them unique from other games. Third-person or "over the shoulder" focused games can get away with slightly less complex guns as most of the time the guns will be further away from the camera and even obscured by the player character at times. Gun concepts in the early thumbnail stages are almost entirely focused on silhouette or "what looks cool"; from there functionality is

TIM MCBURNIE 19/FEB/2014

FIGURE 13.9

Gun concepts by Tim McBurnie. (Used with the permission of Gunfire Games.)

brought in as the designs are refined down to what can feasibly and thematically function in the world (see Figure 13.9).

When it comes to nailing down the functionality of a weapon, an understanding of industrial design or engineering can be a huge boon for a concept artist. The way things are built in 3d is very similar to how they would function in the real world or at least how they may plausibly function in the real world. Large changes to the volume and mass of a rigid item like a weapon when it fires or reloads are strange and noticeable when they occur. Additionally, designs that would require parts to blow through other parts to function in 3d ruin its believability.

Interview

What Are the Things You Would Have Liked to Know about Your Profession before You Started?

Ryan Gitter: It can be a very volatile industry. I suppose I was relatively naive going into it, I played games but was not very immersed in the culture and had no idea of things like layoff cycles, crunch time, etc. I have been somewhat fortunate in that I haven't had a ton of experience with those things, but I've had enough to make me jaded enough to worry about what's down the line.

Christopher J. Anderson: It would have been more beneficial to have learned core concept art techniques at the college level instead of several years after getting into the industry.

What Advice Can You Give for Those Working in a Professional Environment for the First Time?

Ryan: Be friendly, and always try to learn something. Try not to make commitments you can't keep, be honest about how long something will take you, and if you don't know something don't pretend you do. It's perfectly fine to ask questions, but also respect people's space and the fact that they also have a job to do; if you need to ask them something, be polite.

Chris: Study up on how to best survive and succeed in the work environment before diving into one. Much like when children enter school for the first time, there are rules to follow many of which are unspoken and difficult to be aware of.

What Is the Hardest Lesson Artists Coming into the Industry Have to Learn?

Chris: Being honest about the decision to be a concept artist or any title is the hardest lesson. Not truly knowing the solid honest reasons can lead to new workers having a distorted idea about what their role is, what they're really supposed to be doing, and what they deserve. This can and does snowball into major issues years later.

Conclusion

As you can see know, it should be abundantly clear that a concept artist doesn't "just need to draw well." There is a lot more invention and refinement that goes with good drawing skills. Understanding of anatomy, 2d design basics and even some industrial design all play a role in concept art. As with any art portfolio, variety is king and concept art is no different. With every piece in your portfolio you want to establish that you create and invent. Your concepts included in your portfolio should be a reflection of how versatile and creative you are as an artist.

14

Crafting an Environmental Art Portfolio

As an applicant for an environment art position, it is important that you display diversity in subject matter, style, and abilities. As mentioned earlier, the responsibilities of an environment artist take many forms, so you want to show that you are aware of this and reflect it in your portfolio. The ideal portfolio would have several well-crafted scenes that all the major components were created by the individual artist. This means that everything from textures, models, scene composition to lighting was done by the artist. What this would show is that you as an artist are capable of taking a scene from conception to completion. However, as I said, this is an ideal situation, but often not realistic. This is almost impossible to achieve in a professional's portfolio, so it's not expected of an entry-level artist. It's a lot of work, and not everyone is going to be able to knock it out of the park in every aspect of environment art. Also, if you are going through school, it's understood that there will be group projects and much like in the industry itself, a single scene has usually had many people working on it. This makes it very important to clearly label your contribution to the project or individual images.

One thing to keep in mind if you are going to do several group projects as an environment artist, attempt to get out of your comfort zone and try some other things within the boundaries of the job. If you have primarily focused on modeling and texturing, attempt some lighting and scene building. It will give you the chance to grow as well as potentially expand the variety in your portfolio. This will also show your diversity as an environment artist. Most companies look to hire more versatile individuals knowing that priorities and responsibilities shift throughout the course of a game project. Specialization can work in your favor in the short term, but can have a negative effect on your longevity at a company.

From here, we'll be looking at aspects and types of content you should have in your portfolio. Additionally, we'll have some more interviews with industry environment artists and will understand their thoughts on crafting a portfolio as well as other pieces of advice.

Interview

What Makes for a Solid Environmental Art Portfolio?

Melissa Smith: I recognize a solid portfolio when everything in it is awesome, even if it's just a few pieces. The saying that you will be judged on your worst piece is absolutely true. So, if you have 10 pieces to show, but only 2 of them represent your best work. Just show those two.

Laura Zimmermann: A portfolio that contains a few awesome key pieces is much better than a portfolio bloated with too many mediocre ones. Additionally, if you can present an indication that you not only have artistic talent, but also that you're keeping in mind the view and mind-set of the player—looking big-picture—then all the better.

Cory Edwards: Traditional skills. Life drawing, figure studies, still life's and sketches, lots of sketches. Anyone can learn a program like the ones we use to make games. There is no substitute for pencil to paper when it comes to content. Showing a few key pieces is great, but having years of work in your portfolio tells me whether or not you are a dedicated artist.

What Are Some Key Items That Are Must-Haves in a Portfolio for an Environment Artist?

Melissa: Key pieces that get you noticed are things that show your artistic ability, technical skills, and personality. For environment artists, props are great, but environments are better. Seeing how you choose to break down the textures/reuse props/light and the context of the final level/shot provides the artist with lots of opportunities to show off.

Laura: Any examples of assets that were taken from conception all the way through to textured, in-game assets are very important. I think it's also important to see how you can work within game design constraints, such as creating an entire building set that only uses one texture sheet, for example. If you have any concept experience, I think that's important to show in there too—even if it's just some doodles you made on a sheet of paper to prepare you for a larger modeling project.

Cory: Traditional skills, nondigital work, understanding of 3dsMax and Photoshop are must-haves for any environment artist.

Content

When applying for a position it's good to demonstrate that you understand the core concepts behind the work that you will be expected to do. This means that showing examples of what you will eventually be doing. The types of art and assets that an environment artist may be expected to produce are broken out into smaller sections in this chapter. It's hard to make a complete list as every company is different, but it should give a general idea of the breadth and depth of the types of work.

Props

Anything placed in a game level can be considered a prop. This ranges from crates to dumpsters to cars to statues (Figure 14.1). This is the staple of an environment artist's skill set. Often an environment artist will be given a concept or reference for an item and they will be expected to build it to spec. Often this varies wildly depending on the visual style and hardware platform of the game as well as the repetition and importance of the prop. What is "to spec"? What this means is that every prop will have a budget; its triangle count, texture resolution, and sometimes number of materials allowable. How can you represent your prop is at "spec" in your portfolio? The best way is to look at professional artist's modern work that shows the polygon count for a similar object and aim for that. It might not be perfect, but it will force you to think about where you are putting your detail and cause you to practice some restraint. This should hopefully allow you to produce something that is close to the final in game asset.

Attention to Detail Exercise

Previously, we looked at the most common asset in an environment artist's portfolio: the wooden crate. In this exercise, we'll look at a real-world analog to another common 3d prop: the dumpster. Often when a dumpster shows up in a portfolio, it's a "photofit" of a real image found on an online image search. Dumpsters are common in the world, but they make for an interesting 3d asset because they often have excessive wear and interesting texture.

Figure 14.1

An image of one of the most common portfolio props, the dumpster. A–D focus on details that help sell believability in a 3d asset. (Copyright iStock.com/kickstand. With permission.)

A. Most dumpsters will have some rust on them; however, it commonly occurs when the dumpster has been damaged and the paint has been scratched off. In this particular case, there is a lot of rust on the side sections where a trash truck would pick up the dumpster. This frequent friction has worn away the paint, exposing the metal underneath to the elements allowing it to rust.

B. Dumpsters will often be used for the disposal of any number of solids and liquids. So when a dumpster is turned upside down to be emptied, loose liquids will run down the insidewalls, and when it is returned right side up, some of those liquids will be collected near the opening. Over time this will cause collected liquids to begin to streak down the outside. This is a nice element to add a little more visual interest and history.

C. Not all dumpsters have chains; however, on this one, it is worth noting for two reasons. The first is a more general 3d concept. Whenever you have multiple chains on an item in 3d as a visual flare, make them of different lengths. This will help the chains feel more natural and not so perfect. Also, it's worth noting, similar to point A, the chains rubbing against the dumpster have worn off the paint and allowed them to rust. This rust, in particular, wouldn't be there if the chains weren't present.

D. Text and signs on utility type item can help to ground it in reality as well as give it some contextual interest. Also, when adding signs to a 3d object, it is important to "age" them appropriately. In this case, the "trash" sign looks like a more recent addition than the warning signs.

It is important to keep in mind that low poly doesn't mean what it once meant. That's why I mention referencing "modern" professional work as a reference point. I often see portfolios that include "low-poly" work that has what looks to be the polygon count of a PlayStation 1 era game. There are no games that build their assets that way anymore. Even the lowest end phone games are fully capable of rendering many more polygons onscreen than that. However, low poly means different things to different companies; for phone developers, it often means a lower number than a console developer; even then, the numbers are still quite respectable.

Once you have your budget, it's essential to make sure that you apply it correctly. If you're building a car and you give yourself the goal of 10,000 triangles, be thoughtful of where you put the triangles. Obviously, put enough polys in parts that need to be round like the tires, but don't spend your polys noodling on smaller details that could be handled in a normal map or might not even be visible at all. The next important part about managing your budget is your management of UV texture space. While most artists find this work tedious, spending a little more time here can make all the difference in the world when you end up working on the texture. An efficient use of UV space is just as important to making your model look good as the distribution of your polygons. I've seen models that were unwrapped so well at a resolution of 512×512 pixels that they looked higher resolution than a model with poor UV mapping at double the resolution. Also, the importance of a good UV layout can't be overstated, so for this very reason, it's a good idea to show some of your more complex UV unwraps in your portfolio.

When it comes to the presentation of a prop or individual asset, it's ideal to present the prop in a scene it was made for to give it context. However, it's also a good idea, especially if there is detailed high-poly work in the asset, to present it in isolation (see Figure 14.2). This allows the reviewer to assess the detail without

Figure 14.2

Example of prop from *Darksiders II* by Adam Pitts. (Used with the permission of Nordic Games.)

distraction. Presenting both the high-poly sculpt, if applicable, and the final textured asset together also gives the reviewer a good idea of your abilities and your process.

Scene Layout

This has many names and can mean slightly different things at different companies. It can be called world building, level layout, set dressing, or many more titles. This can and often is overlapped with the work that level designers do. Companies can work in very different ways and, like environment artists, designers can have varying skill sets or workflows. Some designers will craft very intricate paper layout maps for a level, whereas others will build levels of gray cubes or nontextured 3d geometry. Some others will take artist-created modular set pieces and craft an almost complete looking level from those pieces. Depending on the company and their workflow, any of these are a possibility. For this reason, it is just as likely the environment artist may get the gray-boxed version of a level, as they may get the final looking version of the level that needs "set dressing" and polish.

Whatever the workflow may be at a particular company, the end goal for scene layout revolves around crafting a playable space that is visually interesting and compelling to play (see Figure 14.3). This is often achieved through guiding the player's sightlines, exploration of space, asset placement, and creating a visual narrative. The player's sightline can refer to where they are naturally led to look or, from a technical perspective, it can refer to an actual draw distance that relates to performance issues. Here, we're talking about the natural direction of the player's view. When crafting a scene, the builder of the scene can never be completely sure where the player may be looking; however, it's usually safe

Figure 14.3

Example of a scene from *Darksiders II: Deathinitive Edition*. (Used with the permission of Nordic Games.)

to assume its forward. Assuming this, laying out a scene you can plan reveals, points of interest, or vistas based on which players will be entering a scene and they must travel throughout the scene.

Another important element of scene layout is the exploration of space. Primarily this relates to the exploration of elevation in a given space as well as changes in the size of the space around the player. Finding ways to add elevation changes adds an element of interest to both the navigation of a space and an opportunity to add interesting visuals that support those elevation changes such as stairs, railings, or decorative items. Size exploration is often accomplished by guiding the player through a smaller, tighter space before introducing a large space to them. This thoughtful application of layout will make the transitions to larger spaces much more impactful and memorable for the player. Additionally it will make the large space feel even bigger than it actually is because of the transition. A practical example of this would be leading a player through a tight enclosed stairwell before opening into a larger ballroom-like space.

Finally, when it comes to a scene layout, asset placement is very important and plays a major role in not only how the player moves through an environment but also what they see while they do it. Often a grouping of environmental assets like a modular set, or a collection of environment assets, will make up the bulk of a given scene. In addition to these, you need key elements or point of interest props that are unique and help give focus to a space or tie a scene together. This could be the fountain in the middle of a lobby of a high-tech skyscraper or an ancient statue in the middle of a forgotten temple. These types of elements deserve to be center stage, and, in many cases, the space should be built around them. You wouldn't want to place these sorts of elements off the beaten path or in a corner; they should be the focal point that makes the whole room more impressive.

Materials

Nailing materials is really important for any modern 3d artist. In previous generations, artists were limited on usable memory for textures, but now even most phones have a plethora of free memory. To put this in perspective, the PlayStation 3 and Xbox 360 had 512 RAM available and the PlayStation 4 and Xbox One have 8 gigs. That's 16 times the amount of memory. However, due to a system processes not all of that is available to the development team, usually about 5 gigs to start with after the system gets its share. That's still a much larger amount that can be dedicated to graphics and texture memory than the previous generation of hardware. What this means is that, in the past, we may not have had the space for specular maps, gloss maps, or even high-resolution diffuse and normal maps, but now that's not a problem.

The lack of memory often meant material surfaces would look the "same." Sometimes, the only materials that were distinguishable from each other were metal versus everything else. Meaning wood, concrete, cloth, and sometimes skin would look like that they were all the same material substance with a different diffuse

Figure 14.4

Example of a gold material lit in a physically based scene that utilizes a diffuse, specular, gloss, and normal map.

texture. Now, through specular masks, specular maps, and even physically based lighting, artists have the memory and tools necessary to make materials look and react to light like their real-world counterpart (see Figure 14.4). It's worth exploring this in your portfolio as it's a crucial element to understand and to be able to produce objects that exhibit these traits in-game (see Figure 14.5). This doesn't really apply to 2d-based games as much, but even stylized 3d games can and are taking advantage of the extra memory with higher resolution textures that show more fidelity.

Lighting

As mentioned earlier, lighting is probably the most important component of any 3d scene. From a visual perspective, it defines your shapes, emphasizes your depth, and

Figure 14.5

An example of a realistic material study by John Pearl.

makes your materials "pop." From a game play perspective, it defines the important elements of the scene for game play as well as highlighting the player's path. While a portfolio environment might never be used as an actual game environment, it doesn't hurt to show you understand how lighting can be used in games. Previously, this could mean putting a red or green light over a door to show the player their goal; however, in modern videos games, the scenes are much more complex and the lighting has become far more nuanced than such a simplistic approach.

Another reason why lighting is so important is because it goes back to the presentation aspect of your portfolio. Presenting unlit or poorly lit images of your work makes it come across unfinished or poorly represented. Even setting up basic lighting can have a dramatically positive effect on how your work looks and how it is perceived and viewed. Setting up a simple three-point lighting rig is a very simple approach used in photography and film that can make your assets look great (see Figure 14.6).

The components behind the three-point system are a key light, a fill light, and a back light. The key light is the main source of illumination for your object and it determines the overall look of the render. If the engine or rendering program you are using to capture portfolio images has a sun light option that can be used as your key light. The fill light is often a light that also illuminates the front of the asset, but that sits at an opposite angle of the key light and is much less intense. It is meant to give detail to the shadow areas preventing them from falling into complete darkness and losing all detail. This can be substituted with a skylight or ambient light depending on the engine or 3d package. Also, in some engines, this can be achieved by adjusting the ambient color of the scene as well if that option

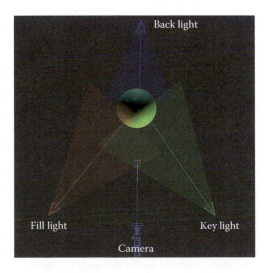

Figure 14.6

A three-point light setup.

is present. The last one is the back light that is sometimes called rim light. It is a light source pointing at the asset from behind; its purpose is to separate the asset from the background and to reinforce the silhouette of the object. Some shaders can fake this effect, referred to as a rim lit shader. This is meant to simulate the effect of the back light, without requiring the asset or character to have a back light on them at all times.

Finally, understanding how lighting works in a game and game engine is an important part of being a well-rounded environment artist. If you are capable of lighting your own work, it makes you a more valuable artist. At most companies, eventually, the need for the creation of assets will slow and environment artists will often begin to migrate over to set dressing or lighting of the levels. It's good to be prepared for these cases.

Modular Pieces

The use of modular pieces to build large worlds isn't a new concept; however, over the last couple of years, it has become the core method for environment creation. Modular piece creation is as much artistic as it is technical. In concept, modular pieces are repeatable pieces of geometry that have a consistent sizing among the pieces and are built to adhere to a particular grid value. What this means is breaking down the structure of a building, hallway, floor, etc. into its repetitive parts. This includes identifying where the best place for a seam to occur as well as finding a logical size to build the pieces to. Some studios use feet, others use meters, some use multiples of 2, others use power of 2, and still others just use whole numbers. If you are going to attempt a modular set, the number size you use doesn't matter as much as making sure what you choose works for the space you are trying to create. For example, making a small hallway that uses 16-m sized pieces misses the point of using a modular set, whereas if you're making the exterior of a large building, 16-m sized pieces might be an ideal size.

One of the reasons why modular pieces have become the standard is because it allows game developers to create a lot of content with a small amount of source pieces. On *Darksiders II,* in a given dungeon set, we had less than 100 pieces for the set that included walls, ceilings, stairs, and floors that we were able to create several unique dungeons from (see Figure 14.7). This allowed the artists to focus on making the areas feel unique through set dressing, lighting, and prop placement as opposed to creating what often turns out to be similar walls, floors, and ceilings, uniquely for each dungeon.

The key to successful modular pieces is to make them repeatable. Much like a tiling texture should be free of uniqueness that visually repeats over a large area, no component of a core modular piece should have any unique parts that don't tile well. This could be but is not limited to distinctive breaks in walls, missing chunks from floors or any accent elements that make a piece stick out as repeated. Those types of unique pieces can be added to the modular set as supplemental pieces and used within the scene sparingly maximizing their visual impact and

Figure 14.7

Example of some of the different environments created in *Darksiders II* using a singular modular set. (Used with the permission of Nordic Games.)

leveraging their uniqueness. Modular pieces are really just the foundation of the scene that allows an artist to quickly put together a level, so the bulk of the time can be spent on the unique parts of the scene.

Destruction

Destruction isn't necessarily a narrative element; however, a lot of games use it in their visual story telling. It's easy to understand destruction; something was once whole; now it's not either through natural or unnatural causes. This is a dramatic transition (see Figure 14.8). Instantly, that speaks to our psyche about struggle, weapons, or change. Destruction is present in so many games, but it is very hard to sell. I'll touch on some of the biggest pitfalls when it comes to destruction in 3d art and how you can avoid them in your own work.

The first pitfall is, "Where did this rubble come from?" Rubble piles are a fantastic tool for a world builder; they allow the artist to instantly add organic shapes in areas like a building interior or a city street where the dominant shapes are straight lines and right angles. At the end of a project that has a lot of destruction, it also acts as a fantastic bandage to problem areas. If there is a weird area where geometry meets, cover it with a rubble pile. If there is a small hole in the geometry, put a rubble pile on it. If the player can't quite make it up to the next of an area, add a rubble pile. It's like figuratively sweeping problems under the rug, but instead it's hiding it under the rubble pile. I present this concept half-joking, but I've seen all these scenarios occur and I am most likely guilty of them myself. Here's why this is a problem: if it's used too much with little context for where it came from,

Figure 14.8

In this image, it's clear where the rubble came from and the materials found in the rubble matches the source. (Copyright iStock.com/tioloco. With permission.)

it can look like someone backed up a dump truck and dropped off the rubble. If a building is completely intact but it is skirted by rubble, the visual story telling falls apart. There needs to be damage above or at least nearby the rubble to make it believable. Also, making sure what broke and the contents of the rubble pile are somewhat consistent. Meaning if a building collapsed, some of the elements that made up that building should be visually present in the rubble piles.

The second most common issue with destruction is, "What is that material?" This happens even within the industry amongst very senior artists; often people get caught up in what they're doing and they forget that different materials break differently. This may come about because it is easy to start cutting and chamfering edges of the geometry all the while completely forgetting the material the polygons are supposed to be representing. When under great stress, materials much like people have very different reactions; wood splinters, concrete crumbles, and metal bends long before it cleanly breaks. This seems like a simple concept, however, time and time again in portfolios, I see wood that looks like it crumbled, concrete that is bent, and metal that splintered like wood. Think about how the material actually breaks and the end visual result will be so much more visually believable.

Figure 14.9

An example of an actual destroyed brick wall. Note how organically the bricks are broken and the shapes change based on the mortar edges. (Copyright iStock.com/Sergei Dubrovskii. With permission.)

This is a minor one, but it's a specific pet peeve of mine: destroyed brick walls. When a brick wall is destroyed, it often comes apart at the literal seams or more specifically at the mortar (see Figure 14.9). However, depending on the destruction type and force, bricks can split and crumble too. When destroying a brick wall and you're low on poly count, it's almost always better to break on the mortar lines unless you plan on blending in a broken texture for the brick edges. Often people will cut a straight line through several bricks, leaving a laser sharp cut through several bricks. This never looks good. In addition to that the broken brick pieces are just as important. A piece that looks similar to the size of a brick should be texture mapped that way; mortar lines running nonsensically down the middle breaks the illusion of the art. Finally, if you are going to offset bricks outward from the surface of a wall, make sure to line those individual bricks with the texture on the wall. Having a single brick offset in a way that allows the viewer to see that it doesn't line up with the brick in the tile of the texture on the wall breaks the illusion.

Attention to Detail Exercise

In this attention to detail exercise, we're going to be looking at the following image (Figure 14.10) and pick apart some of the details that make it up that can sometimes be missed when trying to replicate a scene like this in 3d.

Figure 14.10

An example of an abandoned room. A–D looks at some of the finer details of destruction. (Copyright iStock.com/Pawel_Kisiolek. With permission.)

A. Obviously, the ceiling is missing which left some really cool-looking rafters visible. In a 3d scene, this sort of modeling would allow the artist to go for interesting lighting opportunities as well as parallax as the player character moved through the scene.

B. Floors in a destroyed building in a game are always difficult. Assuming we are crafting a scene like this for a third person game, the floor is the prime playable space. This means that the floor needs to be easily navigable without a lot of obstructions. This is a great example of how one could accomplish this. The base floor peaks through the small rubble and debris scattered about from the collapsed ceiling while leaving the floor relatively flat.

C. One thing to consider when crafting a 3d structure, particularly a destroyed one, is to find ways to add spots of color. Often destroyed environments in games end up being reduced down to gray or brown spaces. This is where the term "next-gen brown" comes from. This often occurs because as things age, they lose their color as well as get dirty, so things can end up pretty brown. Mold or moss is a great way to add spots of color to your scene without feeling out of place. Often destroyed or abandoned buildings will end up getting quite damp because they are no longer protected from the elements of nature. One thing to keep in mind when applying moss or mold is that it will often originate near the ground or spots where water and pool and it will be the most intense near those spots, fading off as it gets further from its origin.

D. It's worth noting the exposed brick here as well as where the floor previously was. This sort of detail is often overlooked when 3d artists create destroyed spaces. They don't consider how the structure would have been built. In this case, there was a wall here as well as ceiling and a floor for the upper level covering the rafters. For this reason, the brick base of the building would not have been painted or plastered like the walls were and is now exposed. This also gives a nice visual breakup due to material and color changes in the walls.

Story Telling

Everything mentioned previously culminates into one thing: visual story telling. Environment art is really about creating a narrative without the use of words through the visuals of the world. This could vary from creating an abandoned army base that has been overrun with aggressive alien creatures to a long forgotten temple in the middle of the jungle.

How does one create a visual story? Often this occurs through the application of props and the path through the space. One of the easiest and most common wins for any 3d environment is layering of themes. What this means is taking an environment and layering a different theme on top of it. Take an overgrown temple as an example; it's not just a temple, but it is overgrown. The temple is the core and foliage is the layer on top. The story this tells is it has been there for long and probably not used in a very long time if nature has begun to retake it. This layer doesn't have to be as dramatic or time intensive as creating a lot of foliage assets. It can be simpler things like creating a location and adding the extra layer that it has been ransacked and left disheveled and scattered. Another simple example is even adding rain or water from a recent rain to a scene. This adds a little more depth and complexity to a scene and grounds it into its own reality. Story telling emerges from the details and lighting. This isn't to say you need a lot of assets or high fidelity in those assets.

The following example from *Darksiders* uses several story telling elements to achieve its final visual result (see Figure 14.11). The application of destruction speaks of decay from neglect, as opposed to a single impact from a bomb or a monster. The oversized spider webs tell a story of a large spider or spiders that now reside in this place. The props include beds, gurneys, and wheel chairs telling the story that this was once a hospital of some sort. The observant viewer may notice the layer of skulls visible through the spiderwebs on the floor. This adds an element not only of horror but also of curiosity of how there can be so many skeletons and who put them there? Finally, the lighting tells the player that this is a cold and unwelcoming place, one of despair or danger.

Interview

What Makes One Portfolio Stick Out More Than Others?

Melissa Smith: In addition to creating technically proficient and beautiful portfolio pieces, finding opportunities to tell stories with your art will encourage people to ask about it. In 2011, Vigil hosted an art show and I wanted to create something new using my skills as an environment artist. A generic prop or a pretty vignette wouldn't cut it. So, I created a piece that people can draw their own conclusions about. I have been asked about it in every interview as well as remembered by it when people recall my work (see Figure 14.12).

Laura Zimmermann: I've talked a lot about variety and creativity, but the technical side is important too. If you're really awesome at doing modeling and texturing, but aren't making sure that your assets are created in an organized fashion, it may come back to bite you. What I love to see is an artist who can not only deliver an amazing asset, but also ensure that the geometry is clean, modeled on the grid when it needs to be, is working within game design constraints, and has nice clean UVs.

Cory Edwards: When you see that an artist includes the work they wanted to make and not the work they think someone wants to see. A great deal can be learned about a person from looking at their portfolio. It's very easy to tell, for example, if someone only shows me class assignments or passed industry work over their own personal work.

Airship by Melissa Smith.

What Are the Most Common Mistakes You See in a Portfolio?

Melissa: A common mistake I see is trying to get "creative" with your website. You are not being judged for your web presentation. Let your work be creative. Keep your website ultra-accessible. Make the art easy to get to, and with little navigation required. Put the art in their face as close to the landing page as possible.

Another mistake is when new artists include student work. Those projects are intended for you to make tons of mistakes on and learn. If you really loved a student piece, revisit it after you completed it.

It's generally not a great idea to post art tests from companies in your portfolio, because employers see many portfolios, and other artists will include their tests. It's easy for a company to draw conclusions when they see similar work in different portfolios that you are showcasing a failed test. If it was successful, you would be with that company and not showcase the test. From that, they may conclude, if another company rejected you, they should as well.

If that's not the enough reason to leave the test out, you will be asked to speak about your work at the interview, in which case, you will have to admit that this was a rejected test from x company; cue awkward silence. Also, I find it's much easier to talk about work I self-directed and I am passionate about.

Laura: Too much of the same thing, or the same style. I don't need to see 20 different versions of gothic architecture to know you can do it. Show how versatile you can be—Sci-fi, fantasy, historical, whatever—show only your best few of each. If you can do other things besides model and texture, even better. If you sketch something before modeling, show that off too.

Are There Any Skills besides the Ones Directly Related to Environment Art Position You Look for?

Laura: I like to look for artists that can carry a concept all the way through from conception to in-game. This industry is seemingly becoming more specialized, and I find it really refreshing to see someone who can still remain well rounded as an artist.

Cory: A strong workflow is something that I look for in a candidate. I'm looking for someone who has taken the time to customize and streamline the programs they use and the things they do all day. Efficiency leaves more time to be creative and productive.

Conclusion

As you can see, environment artists are responsible for creating a lot of different aspects of a game. This level of diversity and variety means that there's room for a lot of specialization within the job. Most of the items that would be found in an environment artist's portfolio are best served as still images. Props, lighting, scene composition, texture breakdown sheets, modular pieces are all best viewed as still images. This allows for a higher resolution as well as it gives you as an artist more control of the presentation. It allows you to really refine the image and try to find any errors in it. If you have built a large scene, a video can be an appropriate way to display your work as well. This can be done through slow fly troughs highlighting the key areas of the scene.

15

Crafting a Technical Art Portfolio

As we've established previously, "Tech Artist" can be one of the broadest art-related titles in games as it can swing from an artist with technical skills to a programmer with an understanding of art to an animator that specializes in character rigs. For this reason, it's very hard to nail down a global "what you need in your portfolio" as a TA. What we'll do is break it down into common types of TAs and presentation approaches for the different types. In some cases, like a TA that focuses entirely on scripting, a visual portfolio website might not make the most sense. In other cases, if you are a TA doing some art creation and scripting, it makes more sense to have a visual component to your portfolio.

In any profession in games, you must "sell your skill set" but in tech art sometimes you're selling people on a skill set they may not realize they need, understand the importance of, or even recognize the positive impact it can make on their project or studio. That's what you need to do with your portfolio. Sell them the efficiency and increased productivity that hiring you would bring to the table. We'll look at ways to attempt to do this with a portfolio. Additionally, we'll speak more with industry TAs about their thoughts on crafting a TA portfolio.

Interview

What Is the Best Way for a Tech Artist to Present Their Work When Applying for a Career?

Ben Cloward: The goal when applying for work is to communicate quickly and clearly that you have the skills that the company is looking for. The skills that you're trying to present often dictate the presentation that should be used. For example, if you are demonstrating that you are skilled at rigging and skinning, you'd use a short video that shows off the best parts of your rigs. If you're demonstrating your skill in scripting tools, you might send a script that you've written along with brief instructions on how to use it. You want to give the company a quick taste of what you can do with the option to see more if they're interested.

Jeff Hanna: Great code samples that are well written, well documented, and clearly solve a problem are what I look for. A 3dsMax or Maya script that cleanly solves a problem and is easy to read and understand shows quite a lot about an applicant's skill set. I can learn about their organizational skills, their communication skills, and their problem-solving skills.

Samuel Tung: Focus on core skill set and build base on that.

Depending on what type of TA position you apply for, you should get your portfolio customized for that specific role. For example:

For a pipeline TA, you should have code examples, workflow charts, and best practices documentation.

For a character TA (technical animator), prepare your code examples, rig setups with video brief, and some animation samples you did for professional work and personal projects.

To apply as a shading TA, you would need a real-time shading examples that you might use a commercial engine or the previewer that you wrote. Show some shader improvements that you did in the past, screenshots with detailed breakdowns.

Some job descriptions are relatively vague, so you would need to find out from the recruiter or asking proper questions to get a better idea. For most of job opportunities, you might have to provide your thoughts and emphasize your strength to get best of offer. The truth is, every studio needs TAs, so be one of the best to help your employer out.

What Can a Tech Artist Do to Stick Out from Other Candidates?

Ben: Probably, the best thing you can do to stick out from other candidates is to build a reputation for yourself. If those that are looking to hire already know who you are, you're much more likely to get hired. You can build a reputation by using online forums and your own personal website.

Be sure that when you interact with others online that you use your real name instead of an alias. If you look for problems that artists are having and then build tools to solve them, and make them available for the community on your website, you'll get attention. If you participate in online forums and help people solve their issues, write tutorials on how to achieve results, etc., you'll create a name for yourself that people in hiring positions will begin to remember.

Samuel: Again, stick with your strength and core skill, and build your stuff around it.

Are There Any Skills besides the Ones Directly Related to a Position You Look for?

Ben: TAs have to be good and getting along with teammates. They have to be able to teach skills to artists without sounding condescending. They have to be able to understand programmers when they describe complex functions of the game engine and then translate those technical descriptions into language that the artists can understand. Above all, they have to be able to recognize, investigate, and solve problems.

Samuel:
- Bilingual, Chinese, and English.
- Chinese painting and calligraphy.

Visual Focused Tech Artist

As a TA focused on the more visual side of the tech art, it makes the most sense to have an art focused. Look develop focused TAs often are capable of creating assets such as characters, props, or even level building. Usually, their focus is on making these assets the highest quality possible, making them efficiently as possible or experimenting with different visual techniques. This could be represented by creating a single scene and attempting multiple different visual styles with it, either through texture application, lighting, or shaders.

In these cases, it's ideal to have images of your results as well as your process. Much like a character or environment artist would give a breakdown of the texture maps used to craft an asset and possibly wireframe images, these are also applicable for a visual development focused TA. In addition to these breakdown shots, any shader, post effects, or other "tricks" used to achieve the final look is important to visually document. Showing your process and workflow is also very useful to the viewer of the work.

If you have made shaders, it's a great idea to include images of the shader network and the visual application of the shader in a game engine (see Figure 15.1). When I refer "shader networks," I'm referring to whatever system in your preferred game engine allows you to create a shader. In regard to the shader network, for portfolio purposes, it's a good idea to make sure that it's clean and readable. Some engines like Unreal Engine 4 have some great tools in their Material Editor

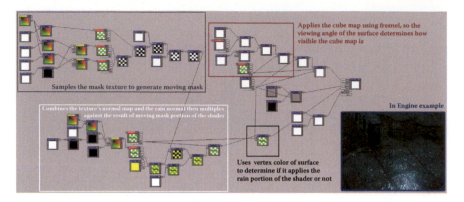

Figure 15.1

Example of a way to demonstrate a shader you worked on. Call out the highlights of the shader's functions and present a final visual result.

that allows you to compartmentalize portions of the shader and label them according to their function. Even if you're not using the Unreal Engine, this is a good idea to do in whatever program you may be using. In cases where labeling tools don't exist, doing it after the fact on the image in Photoshop works just as well. It's really important to show your work just like it is with complex math problems, because shaders are really just math equations.

The other option I mentioned for shader creation is if you're writing the shader code in HLSL, this is a little less visual, but it actually doesn't hurt to take screen shots of particular parts of the HLSL code you've written. Another option is to explore plugins that will display your code on your website with syntax highlighting. Whatever your approach to displaying your work, be sure to point out what you're doing, why you chose to do that, and possibly a visual of the result of the isolated code chunk. Another thing worth pointing out in your portfolio is any HLSL that you've written that simplifies or combines a shader function. Shaders, in particular, ones created using a node-based system, can often be more complicated than they need to be on the shader math side. This is a pitfall of a node-based system because it is so open ended that it allows the user to do almost anything; however, it often doesn't present the user with a way to make things more efficient. What this means is that shader functions are often separated into unique nodes which can lead to chaining several of these nodes together to achieve a result that could have been accomplished more eloquently in HLSL. In these cases, the HLSL-crafted version will most likely be cheaper and more efficient. While this is a little long of an explanation, the point is that if you are putting efficiencies like this in your HLSL, show it off!

Although some of this may seem like overkill, what you're really trying to show anyone who views your portfolio is your level of competence. Much like advanced math classes in school, showing your work and how you arrived there is just as important as the final answer. Explaining why you made choices, or showing how parts of it work together for an end result, shows the viewer that you didn't just copy a shader of a forum or blog. That isn't to say that's a terrible or bad place to start, seeing how other people create shaders and solve visual problems is a great learning tool. However, you really don't want to copy their work verbatim and claim it as your own.

Animation and Rigging Focused Tech Artist

Regardless of scope, style, or visuals, any game with 3d animated characters will require rigging of some sort. Some studios may expect their animators to do their own rigs; while some may understand the value of a person dedicated to rigging. If you are focused on rigging and the animation aspects of tech art, it should be your aim to sell the importance of your skill set. The best way to present this is by showing off your rigs on characters. This can be in the form of images or a video. In addition, also showing some images of the behind the scenes of the rig setup and what makes it better than an average rig. For example, is it the way the controllers are set up, the grouping of helpers, the hierarchy and naming? Often animation-focused TAs will have some scriptwriting skills as well to help them to automate some of the rigging processes or even scripts that allow them to transfer animations from one rig to another. Scripts like this are important to show off in a portfolio and worth highlighting when applying for a job. This can mean breaking down the different aspects of the script and how they apply to your process as well as how you came to a given solution.

In addition to showing off the rig and its set up, truly the best way to show off a rig is to do animations with it. Showing videos of animation tests using a rig and tools you've created is the best way to show off your skills. Particularly, if there are some solutions or automations built into your tools. An example would be if you have written a transfer animation between rigs script, you should show off the most extreme cases of that in action, possibly transferring between a large and small character. Another way to show off your rigging is to show how you've solved the known trouble areas of a rig. On the body, these are the rotations of the shoulders, hip mobility, elbow, and knee bending, while on the face, it can be the area around the eyes and the mouth—any areas where vertices are known to be either of high density or required to bend or fold together.

Interview

What Are Some Key Items That Are Must-Haves in a Portfolio for a Technical Animator/Rigging Position?

Chris Mead: The portfolio should have a diverse set of complex rigging solutions. It should have examples of unique solutions that simplify the animation workflow. The portfolio should have examples of rigs, scripts, and tools.

What Is the Best Way for a Technical Animator to Present Their Work When Applying for a Job?

Chris: The prospective tech animator should have rig files and scripts ready to send for review upon request. Documentation that describes the purpose, best features, and technical challenges overcome for each sample should be included.

What Are the Things You Would Have Liked to Know about Your Profession before You Started?

Chris: It is important to find a studio that truly values quality animation in its games. Quality game animation requires a collaborative effort among animators, designers, and programmers. Unfortunately, many studios aren't willing to commit the resources necessary to make this possible. Certainly, those types of games can be successful, but they can limit your professional growth potential as an animator.

What Advice Can You Give for Those Working in a Professional Environment for the First Time?

Chris:

- Always find the answers to any questions you might have. Don't wait around for the solution to fall into your lap.
- Whenever possible, take the initiative to step up and expand your responsibilities and skill set.
- Always complete your tasks on time. If you find yourself struggling to finish on time or with the desired quality, find someone to help or guide you as soon as possible.
- Always get feedback on your work. Don't just submit it as final and hope that it's up to par.
- Finally, never get too frustrated over work that gets thrown out or of the criticism of others. Take everything as a learning experience and constantly try to improve your skills. Do not overly defend your work simply because you don't feel like working on it any longer. While not all feedback is warranted, all of it should be considered. It's up to the animator how to best utilize that feedback.

Once in the Position, What Can an Artist Do to Grow Their Skills and Mature as a Professional Developer?

Chris: Continue to look for opportunities to work beyond your skill set without putting the schedule at risk. Be prepared to encounter failure, but use it as a learning experience and an opportunity for personal growth. Within your job description, look for opportunities to create impactful work of the highest quality. A project schedule will never allow for every asset to be 100% polished. Pick and choose the best opportunities to create something uniquely memorable. It's also important to review the work of others in the industry and outside of gaming. Always look for ways to improve your work and one of the best ways to do this is to find inspiration in the work of others.

Scripting Technical Artist

As mentioned earlier in this chapter, the goal of a TA is to aid and support the artists on the team through their work. This is especially true for TAs who focus on scripting (see Figure 15.2). As they live in a world between programmer and artist, they are often a conduit and sometimes the only source of tools for the artists if the programming team is small or very busy. When preparing to show off you scripting work, there are a couple things to keep in mind with any tool or script. First and possibly the most important thing is writing a readable, functional code. You want someone reviewing your code to easily be able to read through it and see your thought process and problem-solving abilities. Not to mention it should work as intended.

Beyond writing functional scripts, offering clear and well-written documentation for your tool demonstrates your communication abilities. Documentation is crucial to the success of any tool or script. While some tools created for a project remain undocumented for the course of that project, good TAs will usually create documentation once they finish a tool or at least finish a revision of one. This is important as not only it educates the current team members about how to use the tool but also it benefits any new members who join at a later date or even outsourcing artists who are not in the building. Finally, well-documented tools aid the author of the tool when they come back to update it at a later date. It's surprising how often that comes up and is extremely useful in remembering how and why the tool works.

This may seem like a minor thing at first, but in a game team made up of multiple artists it can end up being a big deal: script deployment. This is twofold actually: the first step is being able to create a menu or icons that function in 3d Studio Max or Maya, though Maya is a little easier as anyone can drag a MEL script into a tool bar. Creating a menu header, tool bar, and entry is that extra

Figure 15.2.

An example of a MAX script interface.

step of usability every would-be TA should consider when working on scripts. Accessibility is just as important as functionality when it comes to scripts. If a tool is useful but not easy to use or access, it will often go unused. The second step of script deployment is that of creating a way for artists to easily install the scripts. As a TA, you need to make a way for artists to easily install your scripts as well as get updates for those scripts. Most TAs will write a python script to deploy their tools. The advantage here is the guaranteed distribution of the tools. If all the artists run it, it guarantees (at least once) all the tools will be installed where they should be and there is little chance of people putting the scripts in the wrong location.

Showing these elements of script accessibility and script distribution tools articulates your understanding of how a TA functions on an actual team. This demonstrates that you don't just have a couple of loose scripts, but that you are thinking of the bigger picture and how the tools you've made will be used in a production environment.

Another element to include in any tool or script is good error reporting whether its robust error descriptions displayed to the end user, detailed log files or a behind the scenes automatic email bug reporter. Including this in your scripts and in code samples shows you understand that while a tool may work in test cases, there are a lot of unknowns once users get a hold of it and you've accounted for ways to track issues in a thoughtful way.

Types of Scripts

Tools or scripts are a solution and without an actual problem to solve, it's often hard to figure out where to start as a TA. This is especially true if you are just starting out and trying to build up a respectable set of useful tools for your TA portfolio. Some suggestions include the following examples.

Creating collision for a 3d object is something that needs to happen for nearly every 3d asset that goes into a game. A script that can automate this ends up being useful for helping artists to get things into the game for testing a lot faster than having to create the collision themselves. In some cases, this automated collision might be good enough for the final collision. In terms of functionality, this could be as simple as creating a primitive that adheres to the extents of a given 3d object or as complex as creating a convex hull proxy for a given object. Additional features for a script like this would be parenting the collision to the visual object and giving the collision an appropriate name. Collision creation and setup are an important part of any 3d pipeline and coming up with ways to streamline this can be a valuable tool.

A common workflow issue encountered on many projects requires an artist to type out or select individual object properties before an export every time they make a new asset. An example of a useful tool would remove the need for typing out object properties and instead simplify the most common properties into groups or a single button press per type of object. This could be in the form of a drop down menu or check boxes. Anything that reduces the likelihood of user input error.

Another type of script that a tech artist might have to write involves scanning large repositories of assets to find specific names, flags, or data types, and then manipulating that data in some way. This is a form of database management which comes up quite often for larger projects. A very simple example would be to search a game's repository for all normal map files that name's end in "_norm" that are over 2048×2048 and to automatically reduce those to 1024×1024. If you imagine looking through hundreds, possibly thousands of textures across a project in multiple unique folders, you can understand the benefit of automating that process.

Another script relating to managing large assets sets involves modular sets. Many companies rely on modular sets to build their environments. The key to any modular set is the position of the individual piece's pivot points. For the ease of use and updates, these modular sets often exist in a single file. Some game exporters expect a single object per file or assume every individual object intends to have its pivot at the origin of its file. In the case of modular pieces, this is not the intentional result. In a system like this, the artists working on the modular file could remember to zero out the object's locations within the file before exporting; however, that is a terrible workflow to do manually. A script solution for this pipeline would be this: at export, move all the objects to the origin of the file, then after export move them all back to their original location. This is a small script, but it can end up saving artists a lot of time as well as avoiding the export of objects with incorrect pivots into the game.

Attention to Detail

In this exercise, we're going to look the interface on a couple of actual scripts and examine what makes them helpful and go the extra mile. These examples are all MAX scripts, but the same high-level thought could be applied to a MEL script

1. The first is a batch folder export. This allows the user to select a folder and then export all the max files in it. It also has a window where it lists out the max files found in the selected folder. This window allows the user to select specific files and just export those.
2. This is actually a dual purpose script that toggles. "Find in max file" toggles to "find in scene" making it extremely useful when searching at the micro (a single file) or at the macro level (the whole project). The window displays the positive hits it was able to find. From this window list, the user can load the file that has the texture they are looking for.

3. This last one is very simple but very useful. It was designed to help environment artists with setting up props for export. Due to the sheer number and how often environment props have to be exported, this script proves to be extremely useful. The dropdown has three options for what it does the pivot of the object: none, to center, to bottom. This is great because the pivot usually needs to be in one of those two pre-set locations. Finally, every object needs to have its forms reset before exporting and this does it for the user as well. Also, it collapses the stack down if that box is checked. Finally, it is the center to world. This can prove extremely useful when exporting assets that don't ignore world space of an individual object.

Tutorials

As mentioned earlier, tutorials are one of the many ways TAs utilize their communication skills. Regardless of the type of tech art career you choose to pursue, tutorials will be a big part of it. This is why it's a good idea to not only write them for tools you may have created but also for processes you have discovered or pioneered. In fact, even tutorials about little known existing tools in a 3d package or engine are a great way to show off your communication abilities as well as showing a deeper understanding with a piece of software package. Having a section on your site, or even links in your online resume is a great way to show off your tutorials. The reviewer of your portfolio may only glance at the content; however, it does leave you looking like a more favorable candidate.

Interview

What Advice Would You Give Your Younger Self Starting Out in the Game Industry?

Ben Cloward: I started out as an animator and transitioned into the role of TA. With that in mind, my advice to my younger self would be to put everything you've got into your work, but make sure that you keep your mind open to what you enjoy doing and look for ways to contribute to your project while doing what you enjoy most.

Jeff Hanna: When I started in the industry, there was no such role as a TA. Everyone was pigeon-holed into artist, programmer, or designer. I'd tell my younger self to not get frustrated because I didn't feel like I fit into the role I was assigned. I'd tell them to more quickly step out and do what felt right in terms of making artist tools and trying to find efficiencies, instead of trying to make do as an artist and not being completely happy.

Samuel Tung: Build your core skill set and expand some bonus skill sets to make yourself unique and add value to the potential employer.

What Advice Can You Give for Those Working in a Professional Environment for the First Time?

Ben: As a fresh new hire, it's really important to be humble. Seek out opportunities to learn from those around you, listen carefully, and write things down. You'll want to soak in as much information as you can and apply it to your work. Don't pretend to know more than you do. If there's something you don't understand, ask about it.

Jeff: Do not be afraid to admit you don't know something. Game development is highly dynamic and constantly changing. I'd much rather work with someone who is willing to ask questions and know their limits than with someone who tries to hide their shortcomings and masks possible issues.

Samuel:

- Ask questions.
- Learn from the best.
- Proactive and self-driven.

Once in the Position, What Can an Artist Do to Grow Their Skills and Mature as a Professional Tech Artist?

Ben: To be a TA, you have to really enjoy what you do. This will often lead you to do your own personal research and learning on your own time. For example, when I was an animator, I taught myself how to use Max script to create character rigs. I did this on my own at home because it was something that I wanted to know how to do and I wasn't getting any time to do it at work. After working on projects at home for a couple of months, I was able to apply them to what I was doing at work. Personal research projects are a great way to learn new skills and broaden your abilities.

Jeff: Write tutorials, submit articles to a publication, and speak at conferences. I cannot stress how quickly a TA can expand their knowledge and their reach by working to teach others. It's a wonderful growth experience.

Samuel:

- Keep learning.
- Discover other filed until you find out what is your true passion.

Conclusion

As it should be readily apparent by now, a TA's portfolio can come in a lot of different forms and focuses depending on the type of TA. There is quite a large difference in duties from look development to scripting; however, they all serve a common goal: creating an environment for artists to accomplish amazing things. It's important to recognize what you enjoy and where your strengths lay as a TA. This should help you to put together your visual portfolio or scripting samples accordingly.

16

Crafting a User Interface Artist Portfolio

Even as recently as the PlayStation 2/Xbox era, UI wasn't a high priority. You can look at some of the early games on those systems and see that. This has changed as games have evolved and the esthetics and user experience have become just as important as other components of the game. Previously, and still to some degree, UI artists come from other art disciplines within games or from outside jobs like graphic designer or web designer. Although games have always had some sort of UI, and really nice looking ones for years now, UI art in games is still a very small pool of talent. This means good UI artists are always in high demand. This is great news for new UI artists looking to get into games. So without working on a game how does one craft a portfolio for a UI artist?

Interview

What Makes for a Solid Portfolio for a UI Artist?

Mike Nicholson: Show good layout skills. This can be web layout, print, or other games.

What Are Some Key Skills for Working on UI?

Mike: In addition to having good illustrative skills, a strong sense of layout is critical. Being able to break down and organize complex information into easy-to-navigate systems is the key to success.

What Makes One Portfolio Stick Out More Than Others?

Mike: We recently had someone on an interview that brought with them their laptop. Halfway through the interview, when asked how they'd improve the *Diablo UI* if they were given the opportunity, they opened it to show us the mockups they had done that addressed that question. Anyone can bring samples; it shows tremendous initiative and confidence to show how you'd improve upon the product you're interviewing for. We were impressed and they got the job.

Mockups

During the course of a game's development, a UI artist on a project focuses on mockups for UI designs (see Figure 16.1), player experience, and overall flow of how the UI works. These are great things to put in your portfolio as these can showcase your artistic sensibilities and design logic. One way to approach this is to fabricate a game with a specific goal in mind: "This is third person stealth game with tower defense elements" or "This is a racing game with a heavy emphasis on puzzles." From that point, think at a high level of what information the player needs on the HUD, think about what's important when they pause the game,

Figure 16.1

Example of an early mockup of the *Darksiders II* inventory screen. (Used with the permission of Nordic Games.)

and think about how they access gameplay from the controller. This may sound silly or even simple on the surface but it can really be challenging. Once you have a couple of fake game ideas, try mocking up a couple of vastly different UIs for those games and pick your best 2–3).

Part of the intent of the mockups should be to show your design and layout skills while the other goal should show off your graphical design abilities. As mentioned previously, a UI artist focuses on ease of readability for the end user. This is particularly important when it comes to the graphic design portion of the UI work. A layout and interface logic flow may be solid; however, if the graphical elements that support that flow are hard to decipher or are trying to display too much visual information the intent of the visuals can be lost. There are games where their UI flow is great but the iconography and the actual UI elements are hard to read. These menus and interfaces may still be navigable; however, this may require the player to mentally map the flow of what they need to get to and ignore the visual elements. This is a huge failure in terms of interface experience and UI artists should work to avoid this at all costs.

Simplicity

Initial UI designs very often start out as large complex beasts, trying to account for all the information the player may need to know throughout the game. This can result in an overcrowded HUD, layers upon layers of menus, and a sea of icons. Throughout the game's development, the UI will get paired down; usually the simplest design and flow will win out in the end. Sometimes it's easy to forget this when you are designing a UI. You as a developer have all the answers or at least a lot of them in regard to how the game works and functions and what's important to the player. The player often knows nothing of the game going in or what the important elements actually are. For this reason, it's important when planning a flow to find ways to bread crumb them along and introduce elements into the UI as they progress through the game as opposed to overwhelming them immediately with too much information. Often the game design will mirror this approach, giving the player a little bit more power, weapons, abilities, etc. over time. All this is done to avoid confusing the player with too much to information upfront. It's good to think about how you can hide these elements or even hint at them in the UI. Having empty spots or locked spots in the UI that looks intentional can alert the player there is more to come but doesn't overwhelm them as they learn the basics.

Icons

Icon design is a crucial skill for a UI artist. Most games that involve loot, spells, or even an inventory the player interacts with have icons. At the bare minimum, even games that don't have these elements but appear on console or on steam have achievements and each achievement requires an icon. What this means is if you're a UI artist, a portion of your job is going to be focused on the creation of icons.

So what are icons? They're just small pictures, right? Not quite. There is a level of graphic design that needs to be applied to the creation of good, readable icons. As they are often rather small and usually square, it's important that like most UI elements they are almost instantly recognizable as to what they represent. Icon design should focus on the form and function and will live and die on its readability.

Icon Exercise

Where do you start with creating icons for a game? Following the steps in this exercise can help you to work through the creative process. In this exercise you will be crafting a set of icons. Choose a type of icon: weapon, armor, achievement, anything really that is represented by an icon. First, think of a single word that describes what you are trying to convey with the icon. From there, extrapolate similar words and find ones that still fit the original intent. Once you have a couple of words, draw out quick sketches of images that represent those words. At this point you can begin to refine the imagery and attempt to find the most readable and relevant images. After narrowing it down to a couple of good images, work on the designs of those, refining the readability and keeping your mind on simplification of detail (see Figure 16.2).

Figure 16.2

Examples of some of the *Darksiders II* armor icons. They are still readable at a smaller size due to their unique silhouette, shape, language, and color. (Used with the permission of Nordic Games.)

16. Crafting a User Interface Artist Portfolio

Figure 16.3

Example the consistency found in quest objects in *Darksiders II*. (Used with the permission of Nordic Games.)

One thing to keep in mind while refining these icons is to use consistent color branding and shape (see Figure 16.3). For a spell-casting set of icons this could mean a fire spell has consistent shades of orange and red in them. For icons relating to items with quality levels, items with a similar quality need to have the same distinct color profile. Consistent shape could mean icons of melee weapons have a similar icon framing and positions that are unique to other types of weapons. In terms of gun-based icons, it could mean all the pistols are turned at a specific angle while all the rifles are positioned at a different angle.

When putting together a UI portfolio and it comes to the icon portion, it's important to show not only icon samples but how you arrived at the icons you've crafted. Show your creative process by walking through the steps you took to arrive at the end results. Show some of the early mockups, sketches, and starting points that lead to your final visual. This is important as it shows off your creative problem-solving skills.

So what should your creative process entail? First off, create a context. If you are not working on a group project, make up a game and try to design an icon set for that. Choose the theme, style, and genre. These are important elements because they should inform your decisions on the creation of the icons. For example, shooters have very different icons requirements than tower defense games do. Thinking about these things before you start should help you to refine down the look and information communicated in your icons.

Once you've decided on your genre, style, and theme, you should start thinking about icon grouping. These groupings would be anything that is similar, like weapons versus pickups versus spells versus creature summons, etc. Group those subsets together and try to find consistent themes within those groups as you brainstorm them. Once you're done with a group, make sure they maintain a consistency in their look.

One thing to avoid when creating icons is trying to convey too much information. Remember that icons are supposed to be readable at a quick glance, so having too much information or too many elements vying for visual supremacy can cloud the actual readability of your icon design. Keep them simple with strong shapes and limit the number of dominant elements. Depending on the goal of the icon, text should usually be avoided in an icon as readability at a small size is often low,

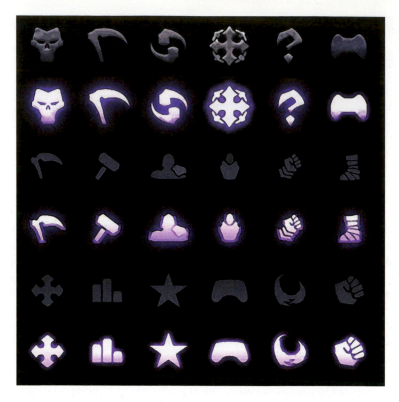

Figure 16.4

Example of icons with active and inactive states used in the navigation screen. These are presented in game very small and are visually readable and distinct in both active and in-active states. (Used with the permission of Nordic Games.)

especially if the UI is meant to be seen on a television. Additionally some icons will have active and in-active states (see Figure 16.4). This means when the player selects the icon or the portion of the UI that the icon represents, the icon must become active to reinforce the player's location within the UI. The design of icons that need to have the two states should be focused on simplicity and silhouette as small details may be completely illegible in one or both of the states.

Visual Language

It's important in a UI to establish a visual language particularly with things the player interacts with frequently but also with things the player hasn't interacted with yet. What does this mean? If the player picks up an item and it is placed in their inventory, it should follow an established visual convention that helps them to identify what it is even if they've never seen it before (see Figure 16.5). This ability to identify the item should be based on their previous experiences within the game.

Figure 16.5

Example of the inventory in *Darksiders: Deathinitive Edition*. (Used with the permission of Nordic Games.)

A health pick up even if it's a larger or better one should follow their visual expectations of the previous health pickups they've received, same with a weapon. The player should be able to tell if an item is a weapon, and if it is, if they are able to use it.

Attention to Detail Exercise

In this attention to detail exercise we're going to look at how different weapon types and their status are displayed to the player in *Darksiders II*.

A. Every weapon has a border on the lower half of its icon where the color signifies the quality of the weapon. This important information that lets the player know at a glance what they might want to equip and what they might want to get rid of. It's important to note the half border as that comes into play in C.

B. This is the player's currently equipped weapon. This has a border that sits outside the allotted space and completely surrounds the icon. It pulses the color of the weapon's quality to call attention to the player that this is their currently equipped weapon at a quick glance.

C. This is the location of the player's cursor. Much like the equipped weapon, it also pulses to draw attention. The key difference is that it has no border outside of the icon; however, the weapon that is highlighted actually has a complete border around it unlike any other weapon on the page. In addition to the complete interior border, there is also an inner glow that pulses. This is meant to draw attention like the treatment of the equipped weapon, but is secondary in importance to what is actually equipped.

D. This is an item that the player cannot currently equip due to not meeting the level of requirement. It is still readable in regard to what it is as well as the quality of the item; however, it is simply red. At a quick glance the player knows this is not accessible to them currently.

Reimagining

Another great way to show off your UI experience skills is to pick a couple of published games you love the UI or you think could use some work. Redesign the UIs in those games. This doesn't mean merely switching what the left trigger and right trigger do, but more of a complete makeover. You might find it impossible as it doesn't work any other way or other ways are vastly inferior. If this is the case, this is most likely a fantastic UI and has a lot to teach you about how it was designed and why it works. At this point, for personal growth it's worth mentally walking through the UI and trying to get a grasp of why it works so well.

When choosing game's UI to redesign, realize that potential interviewers play a lot of games being that they are developers; however, they don't play all the games. For this reason, it's a good idea to pick something more mainstream or at least well known. If you get into an interview, you don't want to have to spend more time explaining how the shipped game functions than your reasoning for why you redesigned the UI elements. It's also important to be a bit humble if you happen to be interviewing at a company that made a game that you redesigned the UI for. The reason is that during an interview, you will likely be speaking with a person who designed the UI. There is always a danger of insulting people if you change their game's UI and tell them how to make it better. Some people won't mind while some people will be completely taken aback, so tread lightly there.

Mods

Another great way to show off your work is to find a game that allows the user to modify the UI. There are a lot of different games that enable the end user to modify the UIs through Steam Workshop on PC. In addition to that, there are often mod communities built around these games that share information, tutorials, and samples of how to get assets into a game. These forums can take some of the guess work out of how to get your own assets into the game. While it's not the same as working on a game in development, you may face similar limitations and challenges faced by a UI artist working on a game.

The other thing about mods is that they give you a chance to check out your work in a game engine. This can expose your design to a level of scrutiny that you can't achieve by viewing it in flash or Photoshop. Additionally, you can post your mods onto sites or Steam, which allow players to use your modifications. Often these sites will have a feedback system built in, allowing users to assign stars and leave comments. This can be a valuable tool for receiving feedback from actual users.

Style

As with all the other art disciplines, variety of style is crucial. For a UI artist, this means being familiar with current UI trends both in game and outside of games, but also able to tackle more traditional illustrative UI elements. Different games have different interface goals and esthetics. Some games have a very modern flat design while others go with a more ornate UI. Being able to work and produce UI designs that run a wide gamut of looks is crucial for sticking out from others who may be applying for the same position.

Interview

What Are the Most Common Mistakes You See in a UI Portfolio?

Mike Nicholson: Oftentimes candidates focus almost exclusively on Blizzard products when showing us their UI ideas. While we appreciate the nod to our work, we like to get fresh ideas and perspectives. We like to see that you're a well-rounded gamer. Show us other games you've played and how you'd improve or change their UIs.

Are There Any Skills besides the Ones Directly Related to UI That You Look for?

Mike: Communication skills are extremely important. The role of UI deals with almost every department in some way. From design to code, art to sound, usability requires several departments to all work in unison to accomplish any given task. Having good personal skills is the key when you're dealing with a variety of personality types spread across multiple disciplines.

What Advice Can You Give for Those Working in a Professional Environment for the First Time?

Mike: Like in life, treat others as you'd like to be treated. Play nice, be fair.

What's the Hardest Lesson Artists Coming into the Industry Have to Learn?

Mike: That working in games is a group effort. Your work will undergo changes you'll never anticipate, so choose your battles wisely. Don't be "that person" no one wants to work with for being inflexible.

What Surprised You Once You Got into Your Position in Regards to the Work?

Mike: UI work is still relatively a young discipline in games. We're a tight group and there aren't many of us out there that can do both art and design in equal measure—but it's growing from year to year.

Conclusion

As you probably can tell by now, there are equal parts of graphic design, creative problem solving, game design, and conceptualization that go into being a UI artist. The key to crafting a good UI portfolio really comes down to showing that you possess all of those skills and selling your communication abilities. While communication is an important skill for every game developer, a UI artist's job *is* communication—not just communication within the game studio but also with the player of a game. All of the work a UI artist does ultimately comes down to communicating both simple and complex ideas in a game through visuals and navigation.

17

Crafting a Visual Effects Art Portfolio

Every part of game development is important; each part serves a purpose. The VFX function in a way where they ground the key scenes and the moment to moment experience of the player. For this reason, when it comes to creating a portfolio, it's a good idea to have a nice variety of "common" stuff as well as some key VFX pieces. Just like every other art discipline, VFX can run the gambit from stylized to realistic. Stylized VFX usually means there's room for some more over-the-top effects in a given particle system. This can come in many forms, from adding unique meshes to more colorful but simplified visuals. It also means playing with common themes and adding a twist to them. This could include unique takes on water and fire, for example, adding more stylized movement to them or simplifying their color and shape.

With realistic VFX, a good place to start is by analyzing videos on YouTube of the real-world analogs to the effect you are focusing on. Depending on the level of realism of the game or the intent of the final product, there can be room for creative license. How far can one take VFX and still consider them real? The best way to describe this is to look at what "realistic" movies are doing. Guns, explosions, and weapons in general are far more dramatic movies than they are in any real-life examples; however, people are completely accepting of what they see in movies and actually will expect it. This means you as a VFX artist have room to exaggerate or push the boundaries even in a realistic environment. The truth is if guns, weapons, and explosions in games were in line with their counterparts in real life they wouldn't be nearly as interesting. As a VFX artist it's your job to make those things exciting and very visually impactful.

What does this mean in regard to creating a solid portfolio? It means you should look at what different genres in games are doing as well as different levels of stylization within those given genres. In a shooter, look at the shots coming from the guns and the impacts those shots make on the environment and the other characters in the game. How does a stylized game handle these things versus a realistic one? What are the differences, and what are the consistent elements. In a melee game, look at the swords or melee weapons, their swing trails, their impacts on the characters and the world. How does a realistic game handle these visuals versus a stylized one? Look at other genres and watch for the visual cues they are using. When creating content for a VFX portfolio, close examination of modern game's effects is a great starting point for identifying how you should proceed.

Interview

What Makes for a Solid Visual Effects Portfolio?

Ryan Rosanky: Personally I like to see realistic VFX and fantasy both at a high quality. And I lean more to those who have the most impressive fantasy VFX. Creating realistic smoke and fire is all fine and good but having the imagination it takes to come up with spells and supernatural effects is very important. Good breakdowns are important and also showing resolutions to problems you've faced if possible.

What Are Some Key Items That Are Must-Haves in a Portfolio for VFX Position?

Jay Bakke:

1. You need to at least match and preferably exceed the quality of VFX in current games. Look the newest high-budget games and make sure you are hitting that bar.
2. Editing for a VFX reel should be tight. For combat effects, the editing should be really quick and snappy. For environmental effects, the pace may be bit slower but make sure you have some camera motion that really features your work, moving or cross-fading from one interesting area to the next without lingering too long. Your top priority is focusing on your best work and cutting out the filler. It's best to think about an action movie trailer style jump cut montage of destruction, combat, magic, and explosions.

3. Don't bog down your reel with shots of less impressive work or older stuff; they can be shown in a separate section on your website if you feel you still need to have it available.

4. *Bonus points:* Demonstrate your skill with fluid dynamics, like turbulence fields, attractors, vortexes, etc.

5. *Bonus points:* Show your ability to combine particles or meshes with more complex shader work like UV distortion, Fresnel, displacement, etc.

Ryan: Good timing, good textures, appealing bloom levels, you don't want to blind people with your effect. If it calls for a bright element add some contrast in there to balance it out. A variety of different stuff.

What Differences, If Any, Do You Feel There Are between Creating Visual Effects for Movies versus for Games?

Jay: Movies use prerendered VFX for a very specific shot. They have to be relentlessly polished to seamlessly blend into a live action scene. They are typically rendered by very powerful server farms because of the fidelity and visual complexity.

Games render VFX in real-time since they might be triggered at any time and viewed from any angle. Because of this, the effects have to be as efficient as possible while still maintaining a cool visual style. It is pretty common for game engines running on a console to have a limit on VFX at about one-tenth of the graphics processer's per frame calculation time. That is a tight requirement you think about all the spells, explosions, and atmospheric fog that could be on screen at any given moment.

Ryan: In film you have a shot planned out from one angle. Your visual effect in a game must hold up in the world from all angles (unless you're working on a side scroll). Also the amount of particles you can have in film is only limited by your render farm. In games you have way less particles but have to achieve the same effect but way cheaper so it's up to you to come up with whatever way you can to make that happen. Also in film the viewer is riding along with the driver of the film. In games it's your job to make the player feel his or her own actions and how they affect the characters and world around them.

Visual Language

A term that gets brought up a lot in game development is "visual language." This can be applied to how the levels are laid out, key elements on a character, elements in the UI, and the style of the VFX. In terms of VFX visual language, it comes down to creating and then delivering a consistent visual message with all the effects. At a fundamental level this could mean all healing effects in the game are green and damaging effects are red. Keeping core visuals like this consistent throughout a game is important as it acts as almost another HUD element for the player. These game world indicators act as reinforcement for the actions occurring on screen as well as reiterating what is happening in the UI. This is a simple example; however, if sometimes healing was red while other times it was green, and in turn damage was treated the same way, it would create a very confusing experience for the player. A consistent use of visual language is allowing visual cues to carry through to every visual effect in the game. For example in a fantasy game, if there are multiple electricity-based spells of varying strengths it is important to keep the visuals somewhat consistent between them so the player instantly recognizes the spell type; this applies to both the color and the effects themselves. For example if a game has three levels of an electricity spell, having the first two look like white lightning and the third looks like red fire would be a bit confusing.

In addition, VFX play a crucial role in providing visual feedback to the player of their impact on the world from dust they kick up when running to blood from enemies they attack to tracers coming from the weapons they fire. All these elements make the world feel alive and dynamic. Often VFX are a great way to add motion to a static environment. Subtle smoke clouds, sparks from dysfunctional lights, drips from leaky pipes are all fantastic ways to breathe life into a world and reinforce the theme of a given environment. These effects are often subtle and not over the top; but the game would suffer without them. They are often an element that goes unnoticed when they are present and done well because they serve the purpose of selling the atmosphere of the world; however, when they are missing, it is quite noticeable.

Visual Effects Exercise

In this exercise you will be crafting a group of magic spell VFX. Pick something elemental or a class of magic you'd like to do. For example, ice, fire, arcane, electricity, etc. Once you've chosen a magic type, create an effect that represents that. This effect can be attached to a model like a sword, a staff, or even to a character's hand. It could be stationary or it could be a projectile. Its location isn't what's important. The goal of this exercise is to craft ascendingly more power versions of the spell. What spell level you start at doesn't matter, but you should have at least three by the end: a weak, medium, and strong version. You can always do more if you find steps in-between that look good.

Ultimately, you'll want to find ways to make particles that fit in relation to each other, like a family, but are visually distinct enough that at a glance the viewer can identify which is more powerful. Some cues you can give the viewer are as follows, using a fire-based spell as an example. A weak fire spell could be just a small fire with a small radius light. Small embers can spark and float off of the effect as well. To step that up for the medium version, it would naturally be a larger fire. The core of the fire can be brighter and closer to white, signifying increased heat. Making the light radius larger and brighter reinforces the power and energy of larger fire. Introducing more motion to the fire itself can signify it gaining strength over the previous lower level spell. Lastly, add more floating embers and sparks falling to the ground similar to the sparks that come off when wielding metal. For the strong version take all those elements of the medium one and crank them up even more; larger radius on the light, brighter, more embers and sparks. Additionally, you can add a fire tornado spin to it as well making it feel extra threatening. Additionally, adding ever-increasing smoke at the ascending stages will help to sell this as well.

Film versus Games

This could actually be called prerendered versus real-time as that is the major difference in the content. However, this isn't completely the case, as even in games there is some prerendering in the generation process of flipbooks and textures. Beyond that, there is surprisingly little cross over between film effects and game effects. That isn't to say there aren't people who can do both; however, their visual goals and tools can be quite varied. The only thing the two really share is the goal of selling cool, believable VFX. In the end, how they achieve this is very different.

With film, an effect's end visual is all that matters; it doesn't matter how it was created or how long it took to create a single frame of it. Even the tools that were used to create it don't matter or come into play. The effect is built for a specific scene or shot and the effect is handled long after the filming of the scene is complete. The VFX in film often have no limit on emitters, fill rate or simulation computation requirements because as mentioned a scene's render time doesn't matter in the end, only the visual result. Lastly, an effect can even be manipulated after the fact frame by frame if necessary.

On the flip side, VFX for games have wildly different limitations. VFX for games need to run in real time, which is the biggest differentiator and means they need to utilize engine-specific particle systems and tools. Complex simulations and long render times per frame aren't possible in real-time graphics because most games need to run at least 30 frames a second. This means artists making visual effects for games need to utilize what game engines are good at which is movement and simulation of sprites, shader manipulation, and utilizing 3d geometry. VFX artists for games work within milliseconds of rendering time, not minutes or hours. In addition to needing to run in real-time, VFX in games need to be "generic" enough to work from any viewing angle and in any environment. While in film a lot "sins" can be hidden as the viewing angle is known as well as controlled, in games the player has complete control of the camera and player movement. One way VFX artists make sure their particles look as they intended them to from any angle is the reliance upon what is called a "billboard."

Billboards are particles or sprites that are set to always face the camera. This allows VFX artists to craft complex but sometimes rather flat effects that feel like they have depth because they always face the player's camera. Examples of this might include flares or glows around a light, a fire effect, or a muzzle flash.

While some game effects are crafted for specific locations or moments, there are a lot of effects that are created to be used throughout a game. These effects have to be created without dependence on the environment to sell the effect. This means they have to look good and be readable no matter where they are used in a game. Additionally, they need to look good without reliance upon lighting; this is why many VFX are unlit or have components that receive no lighting information. This helps to guarantee that the end visual result of an effect is as the artist intended it to look. This also helps with performance as something as dynamic as a particle effect could appear anywhere and it's hard to judge overall performance if those effects needed to be lit.

As game platforms and game engines improve, a lot of work is being done to VFX systems and how they are handled. With every generation VFX in some ways get closer to movie effects, but in other cases get even further away. Most modern engines allow for off-loading some of the simulation of particles to the Graphics Processing Unit (GPU), which isn't even a consideration for film, but does allow games to have more complex real-time simulations. Additionally, as more power in computing is available, particles can collide with surfaces and spawn other particles from that collision. The simplest example would be water dripping from the ceiling. As the water droplet particle collides with the ground, it spawns a puddle as well as a splash effect. Oftentimes in the past, this sort of particle system was possible but had to be hand crafted to the specific location and timed out, which meant it had severe limitations in its use since it would often be built to a specific height so it lacked any versatility.

Character Effects

Unless there is a large VFX team, the work of a VFX artist on a project is split pretty evenly between environmental effects and character effects. First we'll be looking at character VFX. With so many different game genres there is a wide variety of effects relating to characters. This runs the gambit from realistic games with grounded in reality effects to high fantasy games with elaborate magic spells to sci-fi games with exotic weaponry and creatures. When it comes to crafting a VFX portfolio, it's a good idea to attempt a variety of effects that span multiple genres. Each type has its own unique challenges and hurdles. For example a realistic military shooter will often have the challenge of selling believability and matching the viewer's expectations for the effects, whereas fantasy or sci-fi games often need to be believable in that world but often require creativity to craft something that doesn't actually exist.

In addition to exploring these genres, it's a good idea to do some style exploration as well. As mentioned previously, visual styles can range from believably

This is an example of a character that relies heavily upon VFX. The base model is quite simple and the VFX are generating a lot of the detail. Image of War's Havoc form from *Darksiders*. (Used with the permission of Nordic Games.)

realistic to extremely stylized. In terms of realistic effects, they should focus on their realism, plausibility, and fidelity while highly stylized effects will often be judged on their shape language, readability, and color. When attempting different styles, it's a good idea to create a couple of different effects in a given style. This will allow you to demonstrate your understanding of the given style and how to apply to different situations (see Figure 17.1).

Now that we've briefly touched on character effects from a high level in regard to both genre and style, let's look at some more specific examples for those given genres. For a bladed weapon in melee-based game the character will likely need weapon trails and impacts for when their sword or axe hits different surfaces. When it comes to items colliding with surface types, most engines will have some sort of material lookup table. Usually the VFX artist will hook up specific impact effects for each material type. Depending on the game, the surface types can vary greatly; however, the most common surface types would be metal, wood, stone, dirt, and flesh. Knowing this, one could create the impacts for these surface types. This is where selling the world's believably starts to come into play: the way surfaces interact and the effect that comes from that interaction is a crucial part to grounding the world in a reality. A metal sword hitting wood or dirt wouldn't cause a spark; however, metal hitting stone would. This sort of attention to detail is extremely important for any good VFX artist.

Next example is a shooting-based game. A lot of the same direction in regard to supplying multiple material impact types can apply. Bullets are metal and they would impact surfaces differently. In addition to that, they would also leave a visual of where they impacted the surface. In game engines, this is called a "decal." Often a decal is a plane of geometry placed through casting a ray wherever something, like a bullet, impacts a surface. A VFX artist will often supply these decal textures, whether they are a bullet hole, scorch marks, or a splatter of blood.

Environmental Effects

Environmental effects are really anything that relates to the environment or doesn't relate to a character. Some of the most universal are fog/dust clouds, water-based effects, light-related effects, and fire. These can be placed in the level or can be triggered due to actions of the player. In the case of fog and dust, some examples may include ambient fog in the air, dust kicked up from an explosion, or dust spawned from the player's action like moving an old object. These are just a couple of examples of dust; however, from these examples it should be clear that there is quite a lot variety in how each effect would actually look different. In terms of variety, water has a rather large variety of applications. Some examples might be a waterfall, water leaking from a pipe, water rolling over a surface, or even the wake on an ocean or large body of water. Again, these are just a few examples but these are all real-world examples of effects a VFX artist would be handling.

When it comes to preparing environmental effects for a portfolio, including any or all of these examples is a great place to start. The best way to present environmental effects is in a game engine and in an actual environment within that engine. Most engines have default scenes with sample geometry. These are great places to show off your VFX as they give the viewer context as well as size and readability of an effect in an actual game world. Also, another option is in a blank scene as it allows the viewer to focus on your effect and not be distracted by the background (see Figure 17.2). The reason it's so important to show off effects in a game engine instead of a render out of a 3d program is because half of a VFX artist job is quite technical and involves making an effect look good within an engine. This is one of the best ways to show you are qualified for the position.

Textures

Textures are at the core of any visual effect or particle system in a game. For this reason, it's important to be good at crafting and manipulating textures. Understanding how to paint textures isn't required in all VFX positions but being proficient at Photoshop is. At a minimum, knowing your way around the basic tools in Photoshop and how to manipulate textures and their alpha channels is a must. If you are not hand painting textures, you may end up manipulating found imagery and images you've rendered out of a 3d program for your texture.

Figure 17.2

An example of 3 different stages of an environmental effect from *Darksiders II*. (Used with the permission of Nordic Games.)

In the case of using found imagery, it's important to choose the right images and make sure they have appropriate resolution for the effect. In college, my digital imaging professor told us on the first day of class when working in Photoshop to remember the old adage: "Garbage in, Garbage out." This is especially true when it comes to game texture work. Low-quality imagery can't get any better through increasing the resolution or any combination of filters.

Interview

What Are the Most Common Mistakes You See in a Visual Effects Portfolio?

Jay Bakke: Using super long scenes that only have a few effects in them. You don't need to show the 30 seconds of a villain's monologue before he launches the missiles; just cut to the missiles launching and then cut to the explosions. Think action movie trailer, use jump cuts and other quick editing tricks.

Ryan Rosanky: Poor quality of textures, fire and explosions that are just one solid orange color like the smoke particle was just tinted orange to black over its lifetime. Poor timing, weak feeling effects that are supposed to have impact and force. Crazy, expensive-looking VFX with loads of particles to achieve an effect that someone with experience could have made with a quarter of the particles. Don't think we can't tell how many particles you use … we see them all!

What Advice Can You Give for Those Working in a Professional Environment for the First Time?

Jay: It's easy to feel like you are rock star ready to conquer the game industry when you land that first job, only to realize you have a TON to learn when you're actually sitting in front of a complex game engine. Since pipelines for art, design, and code are always evolving, games often end up with some pretty quirky procedures. "Imposter syndrome" is feeling like you are inadequate or don't deserve to be in that position. Don't start to doubt your skills and your ability to learn. Even veterans feel like imposters from time to time when learning new processes. Don't be embarrassed to ask questions and be sure to take notes. Before you know it, you'll be showing those same steps for the next new guy or even teaching a veteran a new trick you've learned along the way.

Ryan: Be humble, hardworking, and polite. Show your work often and get feedback. Criticism is the key and should always be something you want; after all you are building these effects for others to enjoy! What's the hardest lesson artists coming into the industry have to learn? You are not the most talented person in art school anymore…. There is a lot of talent at these studios.

Be humble and learn as much as you can.

Conclusion

VFX can be a very demanding yet very rewarding career path as well as one that is often unknown or seldom taught as a focus in school programs. Good VFX artists are almost always in demand and especially ones that are capable of tackling a large variety of genres and styles. VFX artists are expected to be both technical and creative when it comes to problem solving. Additionally, VFX artists need to be proactive and self-starters in order to be successful at their job.

18

Application and Interviewing

In this chapter, we're going to look at some of the requirements and preparation you should take into consideration before applying to a company. We'll also look at some of the factors outside of your portfolio that actually affect you getting the job you're applying for. Additionally, we'll pose some questions to Lindsey McQueeny, lead recruiter at Crystal Dynamics.

Cover Letter

Cover letters may seem like relic of a forgotten era, before the time of computers and social networks, which in some ways is true. Cover letters may never make it to the portfolio reviewers or even to the hiring managers. However, sometimes they do, and when they do, they do get read. So whether or not they are required when applying for a position may be debatable by some. It's your only opportunity to introduce yourself to the reviewers beyond your portfolio. It's really a chance to let your passion and personality show, so it doesn't hurt to make it somewhat personal.

Actually there is a case where it can hurt if your cover letter is a carbon copy you've sent to multiple companies devoid of any particular passion or specifics. This comes across if your cover letter is very generic and avoids specifics or worse if it reads like it could be for any job, in or out of games. Additionally, it shouldn't be a homogenous, bland wall of text that looks like it was found on the Internet. A good cover letter should really feel like personal letter to a given company. It shouldn't feel like a checklist of buzzwords found on a resume-building site. Sincerity goes a long way and may actually warrant a longer look at your work.

The people reviewing your portfolio—the recruiters, hiring managers, and leads—have a lot of passion for their company, what they do, and the games they make. This doesn't mean you need to stroke their egos. It does present you with a great opportunity to show you've done research and have some knowledge of the company. If you are coming into the game industry fresh, with no prior experience, the personalization of your letter will be even more important. You don't have the experience of shipping games or working in a studio to rely upon, you only have your work and your personality to sell yourself to a company. It's always good to put your best foot forward in both regard.

The flip side of that is getting those "facts" wrong. It comes across as bad if not worse than a generic cover letter does. As a hiring manager receiving a cover letter with a submission and seeing a different company name in the letter or referencing a game the company didn't work on is a little off putting. This has happened more times than I can count so it has to be a relatively common occurrence, and is actually quite an easy thing to avoid.

Anyone will tell you it's important to tell the company you are applying to that you would be excited to work for them. However, it's crucial not to stop there. If you are truly excited to work there, describe in some detail why you are excited; is it the company's legacy of games you've enjoyed, their unique artistic style, their memorable stories, their upcoming game, an article you've read about the company structure? What is it that actually excites you about them? This is your opportunity to show you are truly engaged and put some thought into the letter. If it's a newer company or they haven't shown what they are working on yet, do a little legwork. Most likely you can find out something about the company online, either through their website, LinkedIn, or many other search results. After all of that if you still find yourself struggling to find something that excites you about the company beyond "looking for a job," you might reconsider applying there at all. As mentioned in previous chapters, passion is a core tenet of game development. If you don't feel an excitement about a company, it will come across in your interview, if not your cover letter.

If you are excited to work for a specific company, it only takes a few minutes to Google them and read through their "about" page on their website or find the most recent news story about them. It's understandable that when you're preparing to submit a portfolio to a lot of different game companies, that seems like a lot of extra time. However, if you expect someone at a studio to take the time and review your work for a few minutes, shouldn't you take the extra couple of minutes if it meant your submission stood out just a little bit more?

The second crucial element everyone will tell you is important to include in a cover letter is selling your skills or describing why you believe you would be an asset to a company. Again, this can and should be catered to the specific company as well as tied back into the work in your portfolio. This means if the company has a particular art style that is similar to work in your portfolio, reference that. If you worked in a particular game engine that you know the company works with, mention your experience. If there are particular skills or responsibilities that you can reference in your portfolio or elaborate on a previous experience, highlight those things.

Cover letters are often looked at as a formality when applying to a company, usually because it's seen as the only unique element to consider when sending a lot of applications out. This could be why they are treated so unenthusiastically—one last hurdle before blasting out your portfolio. You should look at it as a unique opportunity to introduce yourself as well as show them you are truly interested in a company for a career and not just for a paycheck. Taking an extra 10 minutes to write a unique cover letter may mean getting your foot ever so slightly in the door. Remember, as mentioned earlier, if you're struggling to find the 10 minutes or something specific to say about a company it's probably not worth applying to them.

Interview

What Makes for a Solid Portfolio?

Lindsey McQueeny: "Solid" portfolios are just that a fully realized, user-friendly place that really tells a strong story about your skills, experience, style, and process. The best portfolios have something for every type of viewer ("viewer" being the key word here, your portfolio should show, not tell, wherever possible or appropriate). Your latest and greatest work should be the first thing anyone sees when they click on your link. But then the option should exist to dig deeper. If you are a game designer, for instance, where can I see levels you built or game play in action? Am I able to find a link to play your game somewhere? How about some videos with some explanation on your contributions? How about a whole other page devoted to your process, what you learned, how long it took you? Is there another tab for old things you've done and the lessons you learned from that? How far have you come in your education, career, or personal projects?

It should be noted that portfolios these days should be digital, preferably living online somewhere. You would never want your hard copy portfolio to end up in a box somewhere because it has to be stored somewhere—practically speaking, most game companies don't accept hard copies of anything anymore just for that reason, since legally those have to be stored for in some cases a few years.

What Makes One Portfolio Stick Out More Than Others?

Lindsey: I can answer this question two ways. The reality is the portfolios that stick out more often than others are the poorly executed ones. These are the ones that haven't been updated in years, the links don't work, they do more telling than showing, the interface isn't friendly, the information isn't useful or convoluted … you get the point.

To make your portfolio shine in all the right ways; my best advice is to get advice. Put this in front of the people doing the job you want to do and ask them, "Would you hire me based on this?" and ask it without the agenda of actually looking to get a job. You'd be surprised how receptive people are to helping when you are on an honest quest for self-improvement.

My practical general advice though is that the portfolios that shine the most are the ones where you can see the application of those skills to solve resource needs at the company. Not all skills at all companies are created equal so, to the best of your ability, make sure your portfolio is speaking the language of the company you are applying to or at least explaining away the gap and wider application of your skills if it doesn't.

Are There Any Skills besides the Ones Directly Related to a Position You Look for?

Lindsey: This is going to be studio-, team-, and project-specific. Some studios will need people who are more generalists, while others more expertise driven. Smaller studios will need people who can work more independently and without a lot of oversight, others will be more team driven and will require a person to be easy to work with.

Soft skills aren't easy to sell to someone on paper, but are definitely the skills necessary to make games, because there's always an end user to whatever you are doing. The ability to communicate appropriately and effectively to your target audience is probably the most important soft skill of all for that very reason, whether your audience is your teammates, your business partners, or the people actually playing the games you are making.

What Are the Most Common Mistakes You See in a Portfolio?

Lindsey: The basics are the most common—not having a fully realized, error-free portfolio, which is easy to use and showcases your best work. I think the thing to remember is that a recruiter or hiring manager may only spend 30–60 seconds glancing through a portfolio and moving on if it isn't very interesting from second 1, so you want to make every second count.

Social Networking

Your online presence is what others perceive you to be if they haven't met you. This might be great in high school or college if you're trying to groom a cool persona; however, when applying for a real job this "cool persona" will often not be seen as such by companies you are applying to. Realistically, many recruiters and hiring managers will do some cyber sleuthing on potential candidates. This can be LinkedIn, twitter, Facebook, Instagram, Polycount, DeviantArt, etc. What this means is you should be conscious what you post on these sites, or if you really can't control yourself, it's better to set all these profiles to private. Aside from that, use these sites to their fullest potential or take advantage of what they were designed to do.

Twitter

Twitter, for example, is a great way to follow people in the game industry in a more casual atmosphere. Game developers often post about games they're playing, cool art they've found, news about their company, or games that they're working on. This avenue is a great way to see cool stuff you may never have heard of and see a more intimate view of game development life, 140 characters at a time.

Art Forum Sites

Polycount and similar art forum focused sites are fantastic resources to see what other artists are doing as well as getting feedback on your own work. There are a lot of professionals who frequent these sites and will often provide very insightful and concise critique. Additionally when they finish a game they will often do a collective "art dump" of the game's assets. They will usually post their textures, Zbrush sculpts, and isolated assets. This is a great place to get inspiration for your own portfolio presentation as well as compare your own assets to professional's, and hopefully learn some new tricks or even ask them questions.

In addition to sharing your work and viewing others, these sites will often have a forum dedicated to job openings. The posts found in these forums are sometimes collected by the users who are scraping all the major company sites regularly. While other times, recruiters from a company may post directly there. Whatever the case, these types of forums can be particularly useful in the job search.

LinkedIn

LinkedIn seemed to take off in game development earlier than it did in most job sectors. This may be due to the extreme volatility and the frequent turnover rates in games, as it's always proven difficult to keep in contact with former colleagues when they leave a company or the company closes. LinkedIn enabled game developers to do just this. If you don't have a LinkedIn account, you should probably set one up. LinkedIn has proven to be just as important as having a resume in the job search market. Oftentimes when applying to a company, a recruiter or portfolio reviewer will do a quick search of your LinkedIn profile. Also, based on your connections and key words in your profile, recruiters may contact you directly based purely on your LinkedIn profile.

When using your LinkedIn profile, it's important to remember, it's not Facebook. Even though LinkedIn has begun adding birthday reminders and encourages people to post articles, it's still not Facebook. It's important to present yourself as a professional on LinkedIn, if you're looking to get hired. Even worst case if you don't have any work experience to put on your portfolio, it can act as singular location for your resume, contact info, and a link to your portfolio as LinkedIn pages often are the top of a Google name search. It's also important to keep this information current and relevant. If you've moved your portfolio site or learned some new skills, update your resume and your LinkedIn profile.

It's important to remember LinkedIn is not Facebook. Did I say that already? Yes, but it can't be overstated. Posting nonjob/career related stuff on your profile is a big no-no. It's the quickest way to get people to un-connect with you on LinkedIn. Most people come to LinkedIn to see people's new jobs, job postings, and industry relevant news or to message colleagues, and not to read posts that belong in a more casual atmosphere like Facebook.

Beyond having a profile that doesn't have a lot of contacts or experience to list, what is the advantage of setting up a LinkedIn profile besides having a "presence"? This is a good question. Most game companies have a "company page" where they will often post job openings even before they show up on other job posting sites. In addition to this there are groups for particular job types on LinkedIn where recruiters will post directly and similarly skilled individuals will post helpful information. If you find the groups that are relevant to you, joining them will make them show up in your feed. Lastly, company recruiters are on LinkedIn. You can search for companies you are interested in working for and connect with their recruiters. Doing so will allow you to see their updates on positions as they open up and any news the company may share. This can be particularly useful if there are no openings suited to your qualifications immediately.

Application

Once you have your portfolio, it's time to apply, but how do you know who's hiring? When looking for a job there are numerous sites out there; Gamasutra has a great jobs section, LinkedIn as mentioned in the previous section, and art forum sites like Polycount have a jobs posting forum. Also, don't forget to check a company's website. Some companies will post on their website first before posting elsewhere. Often sites will have a jobs section and even if they currently have no openings they will often post an email address to contact and submit portfolios to.

When applying to a company it's important to be confident, but humble. What I mean is, know what "you" are applying for. The worst way to start an application or cover letter is, "I'm looking for any job openings you might have." I don't know if this is taught in school as a valid tactic for getting your foot in the door but I can't imagine it works very often. Game development and its disciplines require such dedication and specialized skillsets. There's no one who is good at all of them, so really "any job" wouldn't actually be possible. I'm not really sure what the intent of the "any job" application is, because it comes across as somewhat naive and uniformed about the realities of game development. It is also a bit dismissive of all the hard work that goes into refining a specialized skillset as well as the company you are applying to. The only variation on this that is reasonably acceptable is "I'm an environment artist who also does concept work" or "I'm a character artist who rigs characters as well." That is very different than the "any job" claim because it is calling out very specific skillsets. Those specific skillsets, assuming you can actually do them, are quite valuable and someone with these multiple skills could fit in any development pipeline quite well.

Realistically, when you are applying you should have a portfolio and you should have chosen an art path. If anything, hopefully this book has shown you that it's important to pick a skillset and refine it as opposed to dabbling in a little bit of everything. In regard to applying, you should know what job you want! Ask for it. Start out with confidence by stating the job you are applying for and at least the person reading it will know what you want and can view your portfolio as such. Once you decided on the companies you will be applying to, take the time as mentioned previously, and write a personal cover letter to each.

Interview

If You Could Give One Piece of Advice about the Application Process to a Game Studio, What Would it Be?

Lindsey McQueeny: There are "so many" but if I just had to pick one, and make it practical, I'd say make yourself a checklist of to-dos when applying to a position, and go through them. Did you test your portfolio with a few people, developers, friends, family to make sure it's user-friendly, error-free, and looks presentable? Did you write a cover letter particular to the job and position you are interested in? Did you get the company name right? Did you follow-up after you applied somewhere if you haven't heard back? Do you know anyone who can help make an introduction? I would do this for every position at every company you apply for.

What Are Some Common Mistakes Candidates Make When Interviewing?

Lindsey: I think the biggest mistake is the mistake of taking it personally. Applying for jobs when you don't have one or really want that particular one is definitely something to take personally—but I think it's important to keep things in perspective. Assuming the company is viable and looking to hire, they "want" you to be awesome so that they can hire you. But the hiring process can be as loaded, mired with politics, timing, budgets, and convoluted with process and red tape for the people who want to hire you as much as it is for you who wants to get hired there. At the end of the day, making games can be as much business as it is passion, or even more so, and it's important to remember that when you are feeling disheartened. It could actually be an "it's not you, it's me" kind of situation.

Complacency or thinking yourself above the process is also a common mistake—for someone at entry level, it shouldn't even be a question that you are willing to write a cover letter or take a test or show more work, and you should be constantly self-improving, with or without a job, because that's the nature of both a highly creative and highly technical industry. But even as you move up the ranks in your career, games are made through urgency, innovation, process, and finding solutions—in essence, making games is one big test. And if you aren't willing to go through the steps in the process, such as taking a test, then that doesn't bode well for the test of working with a team to make a game every day. I've had more seasoned people get offended with being presented with having to take a test as a part of the process, to which I reply: number one, it isn't personal—it's the law. If I test one, I must test them all. Number 2, everyone in here in the same position, therefore, has taken that test no matter how "seasoned" they are. How we do things here, our process, style, expectations of quality, speed, these aren't created equal across all studios. We're special in our own way, just like you are, and there needs to be mutual respect when it comes to assessing that equation.

Practicing is also huge. "Interviewing well" is actually a skill all by itself, and not one that comes naturally to most. And like most skills and talents, practicing is necessary to grow and maintain. With so many widely available resources out there, there's no excuse for being unprepared.

It's also a mistake not to ask questions. Besides actually learning what you want to know, asking questions is a way to get a company to engage with you and therefore leave a more lasting impression. Plus, it's about doing your own due diligence—we are thoroughly checking you out to make sure you are a good fit. You should be doing the same to make sure the company is a good fit for you.

It's a best practice to follow-up. I wouldn't say it's a "mistake" if you don't, but it is at least a missed opportunity if you don't. Saying thank you for someone's time leaves a good impression if nothing else, and if you didn't get the job you can also take that opportunity to ask for help or feedback. Maybe you'll get it, maybe you won't, but at least it shows you care.

Persistence

Persistence is a good thing but there is a fine line between being persistent and being annoying. It is completely acceptable at any stage in the application process to contact the recruiter you have submitted your sample to or have spoken with previously. After you do your initial submission via the company's website, or the jobs email it's not a bad idea to send a follow-up email. This shouldn't be a day or even an hour later, but anywhere from a couple of days to week is a good amount of time to pass before contacting them. This follow-up can be used to confirm they received your submission and to show your level of interest in the position. A week is a good amount of time because people can be on vacation, out of the office, or just really busy on any given day, so that allotted amount of time passed can usually negate those things.

What you don't want to do is continue to send follow-up emails after the initial one if you haven't received a response. At that point it's better to let it go, or give it another week or more before sending another email. There is always the off chance the recruiter has been out for a very long time and the email box has a large backlog of emails, or in very rare cases the recruiter may have left the company. Realistically, no more than two unsolicited follow-up emails seem to be the line between persistent and annoying. If you receive no response, it's best to assume they are not interested. They may reply at a later date, but for your own sanity, it's best to leave it after the two and move on. It's easy to slip into a mode of, "If I keep contacting them, they will see I REALLY want the job." Remember that's not the case and may actually cost you the job.

Lastly, a big no-no, which I've actually seen happen with some frequency, is to attempt to contact the recruiter directly through their nonwork-related social media accounts like twitter direct messages or Facebook. I'm kind of on the fence about even contacting a recruiter through their work-related social media accounts, like LinkedIn, after you've applied. If you've submitted directly to a recruiter through a company's site, it may or may not be ok to contact them through their LinkedIn account. This is entirely up to the individual recruiter's personal feelings on the subject so treed very lightly in this domain.

Art Test

Art tests have become very common place in the game industry even for mid-level and senior positions. As an artist starting out, don't be taken aback or frustrated that they are asking for an art test. It doesn't mean your work isn't up to snuff; it often means they like your work but want to see something more specific from you or see how you handle a task from beginning to end. When reviewing a portfolio it's almost impossible to tell how much time has gone into something, how many revisions, and what parts were intentional decisions.

Art tests often can be extremely specific and very vague at the same time. Often the specifics come into play with technical aspects, subject matter, and sometimes style. The vagueness can come into play with particulars like details, look, and level of polish. The reason for this vagueness is that the reviewer is often looking to see what the candidate is capable of inventing and extrapolating from open-ended direction. As an artist this is your opportunity to wow them and show your stuff. The little attention to detail and any unique elements you add will make your work stand out from other candidates.

Some 3d art tests can be very specific and have a concept they expect the artist to produce in 3d. In these cases it's important to pay close attention to the concept and its details. Often the concept provided for art tests is chosen because it parallels specifics for their game and tests skills they are looking for in a candidate. In these cases it's important to take note of things like specific material call outs, shape language, color cues, and proportions. In some cases, if the company's game has been announced it's pretty easy to understand what they are looking for; again, this requires you to do a little research on your end. If the company hasn't posted images of their game or is a completely new company it may be hard to figure out what they are looking for. It is completely acceptable to ask questions when you receive the art test. This seems like a no brainer but it happens; don't waste their time by asking questions that are actually found in any documentation they provide you. It's a waste of time for them and can make them think you are very bad at following or understanding directions. Ask thoughtful questions that will allow you to do a better test and be more successful with the end result.

Some companies choose to be very involved in the art tests, requesting the candidate send updates at crucial points in the process and even providing feedback on those submissions. Other companies are quite hands off and just expect to see the results at the end. Oftentimes if the company has a specific process they want you to follow they will include it in the description provided with the art test. Additionally they will specify a time frame expectation and delivery format.

Art tests are really important but they can also be extremely time-consuming. If you apply for multiple jobs at once, there is the chance you may hear back from several companies at once, all expecting you to complete art tests. At that point it's really up to you to decide which ones you want to do. It's completely acceptable to push off art tests from one company to work on another. Just be up front that you won't be able to start a test until a certain date you can choose, if you want, to tell them this is because you are working on another art test. Remember you don't have to tell them that.

Phone Interview

Phone interviews are often the first step in the interview process for any job; game jobs are no different. Depending on the size and structure of the company there may be a single phone interview or a number of separate ones. If there are more than one, often human resources or a recruiter will contact you first. This will sometimes be what they call a phone screen.

A phone screen usually consists of the same or similar questions for every candidate for a given position. These questions can pertain to experience, qualifications, and sometimes salary. This is usually the second step in the hiring process as the first step involves the recruiter, human resources, or team leads sorting through all the applicant's portfolios and choosing which ones they'd like to follow-up on. This call is referred to as a "screen" because it is often meant to act as the second filter of the process to eliminate unqualified candidates and save the team leads and directors the time of speaking with every candidate.

As the candidate in the call, the most important thing for you to do is to be prepared for the phone screen. This sounds obvious; however, many people are not prepared and this can come across as disinterested in the position or underqualified for the position. The questions most likely will be about you, your experiences, your job expectations, and your work. Some questions may be very specific about a particular piece in your portfolio or experience listed on your resume. If possible, it's a good idea to be at a computer with your portfolio and resume open when you take the call. Don't think of this as cheating. Often when put on the spot people seem forget specifics of their own work or even what they've listed on their resume. Again, this can come across as poorly prepared on a phone call. Additionally it's best to eliminate distractions when you are on a phone interview. This means putting loud pets in another room, asking for some privacy from anyone else who might be nearby you, or not walking on a busy street. Oftentimes people think the best way to get some privacy or quiet is to step outside, which can work unless it's a busy street or a windy day. I've had to ask a couple of candidates to please step inside or into cover away from the wind because the background sound was drowning them out.

As much as you will be answering questions, it's a good idea to have a couple of your own ready. At this point, these should be general questions the person speaking which you should be able to answer: things about the company, culture, or team. It's in your best interest to do some research on the company before speaking with them; this will allow you to ask more informed questions. These questions shouldn't be outside of their wheelhouse, like asking the human resources representative, "What version of Zbrush is your studio using?" or "What software do you use for burning down high poly models?" Save those questions for the follow-up interview with an artist on the team.

If you have recently gone through school, expect questions about that experience, about the program you went through, working with others on projects, and any challenges you may have faced along the line. If you have listed working somewhere other than games on your resume, don't be surprised if that comes up. Often the goal for this screen is really to find out about you, particularly your work ethic, capabilities, and competencies. Once these have been established, if they deem you a good fit for the position they will often schedule a follow-up call with a lead or director from the team to ask more specific questions about your work and yourself.

Interview

Can You Describe the Purpose and Expectations of a Phone Screen?

Lindsey McQueeny: "Phone screens" mean different things at different places. A phone screen is typically a basic overview chat that breaks the ice and covers the basics. You should be as prepared for that call as any in the process, so know your audience, know about the company and job you are applying to, and be ready to speak to your situation: your status, skills, experience, and goals.

The best thing to do is just ask what to expect. Is this just to talk about your general status and expectations? Should you be prepared with anything beforehand?

What's the Toughest Interview Question You Like to Ask and What Sort of Response Are You Looking for?

Lindsey: What's your biggest mistake you've made in your career so far? What did it cost you and/or your company? My expectation is that people are open and honest about their own areas of growth and learn something from them. Failures are often a bigger opportunity than successes and seeing what came come from that is very illuminating for an iterative process such as game development.

What Questions Are You Looking for Candidates to Ask in Interviews?

Lindsey: The expectations of the role, the studio, the goals of the company, the strengths and weaknesses of the team—having no questions at all is a missed opportunity.

What's the Best Question a Candidate Has Ever Asked You?

Lindsey: Why aren't people successful at this company? Where does the biggest misalignment of expectations come from?

Rejection

Unless you have an "in" with the company you are applying to or you are the best artist in your field you will deal with a fair share of rejection. Realistically even in those two scenarios, the job is still never guaranteed. The key is to never take a rejection personally.

Rejection is hard at any point in your career and can be especially disheartening when you're starting out because you're going to hear a lot more "no's" than "yes's." It can be even harder if you've gone through any of the steps of the interview process, especially an onsite interview. At this or at any point in the interview process, it's important to remember there are many aspects in play when a company is assessing candidates. Interviews are rather short; even a day long onsite interview isn't long enough to truly gauge a person's abilities and personality. For this reason alone, it's important to remember that it's not always something you did or something you said.

I have seen many cases where it had nothing to do with the candidate and it was entirely internal to the studio as to why they had to pass on a particular candidate. These scenarios happened anywhere from the initial submission of the portfolio to just short of sending an offer letter. To provide a little more insight into actual scenarios, I'll list out a few. The company or their parent company released a game recently that failed to meet sales expectations and because of this the current game's budget needs to be cut or they have declared a freeze on hiring. The person who the new hire was meant to replace decided to stay with the company and the position was no longer available. Someone internally from another department or sister studio filled the position. Another candidate who the recruiters assumed was passing decided to accept the offer. The list goes on and on. This is meant to serve as a reminder that it's not just you and the open position; there are other candidates and other circumstances that are completely out of your control.

While these are all possible things occurring behind that scenes and usually without you being made aware of it, at the end of the day it is still up to you to put the best "you" forward in any step of the interview. Perception is everything in an interview, so it is important to think about the "you" that you are presenting.

We've looked at some internal circumstances that can stand in the way of you getting a job, let's look at some hidden factors that often won't be completely obvious in how they affect your chances but are completely in your control.

Attitude

Attitude is often the biggest influencer when companies are weighing potential hires. What does this mean for you as an applicant? This "attitude" that they will be assessing will come in the form of how you speak about your work, video games, and the company you are applying to. What they are looking for is passion without rigidity. A positive outlook on your work, art, and the industry in general will go a lot further than a negative or disinterested perspective. This may seem obvious, or asking you to "be someone you are not"; however, it is crucial and can make or break an interview. Many people are nervous when they interview, and this can prevent their true personality from shining through. On the other hand, I have seen people who were too comfortable and were convinced the job was theirs and they were a bit loose with their opinions.

Unfortunately, I don't have a magic bullet or "one trick that makes all interviews easy." Really the best advice is, again, to be confident but humble. If you are speaking with a game company they obviously see some potential in your work and are interested in you. That is exciting; use that excitement as your catalyst during the interview. At the same time, it's important to remain humble as the people you are being interviewed by have many more years of game development experience than you and you should respect that by not acting arrogant or like a know it all. When asked in an interview if you know about something or how to do something and you don't, say that. Be honest about your knowledge and engage the interviewer about a subject you don't know about so you can learn.

Work Ethic

Often interviewers will try to gauge your "work ethic" by asking about how long a piece took, how you approached the piece, or if it was a group project, how was it to work within the group. Work ethic is extremely important as the job of a game developer can be stressful and requires you to work with a number of different personality types. Additionally they need to find people who will be able to stick with it and not give up easily.

Another easy way to prove this silently is to not have a lot of work in progress pieces in your portfolio. Realistically, in a portfolio the most work in progress (WIP) for short pieces you should have is 1 or 2. If you have no intention of ever returning to it or it's not very far along, it's not really worth including. It's a bigger detriment in the end, especially if it comes up in the interview. That isn't to say you should never post unfished work online. There are fantastic resources and forums out there where you can receive critiques and feedback throughout your entire process. A portfolio is not really one. One of the only times I personally appreciate seeing a WIP is if it's the most current piece and the artist is actively working on it. I think those actually make for a great conversation piece in an interview. These, unlike older WIP pieces, are fresh on the artist's mind and they will often have a lot of energy and stuff to say about them. Also, it is a good way to show the most up to the minute artistic progress you are making.

Cultural Fit

This is a big one and it is one of those "it's not you it's me" situations to a degree. A company may not perceive you as a good cultural fit, which can lead to rejection. While the other items are directly in your control, this one is not as much and can be based on your attitude and work ethic. This is to say it's how they perceive you in an interview. I can give an example where I almost missed out on my first job because they didn't see me as a good cultural fit. I showed up to the interview in a suit at what was a very casual game development company. One of the guys who interviewed me originally later said they really liked my work and knowledge of modern games but were a little worried because I showed up in a suit. This was more than 15 years ago and I had been told by my parents and teachers that a suit was the best way to impress people and put's your best foot forward. Suits were as far from my normal wardrobe as possible, but I was just starting out and was taking any advice I could get. Lucky for me, the suit didn't ruin my chances but it completely changed the perception of the people who interviewed me. So the morale of this story is being aware of the presentation you are making and how it will be perceived. Also, more specifically, don't wear a suit to a game job interview. At the most wear a polo shirt or a nice top, but not a dress shirt with a tie or a dress. Game development is so casual that you should wear the nicest version of what you would normally wear in your day-to-day life. I only caveat it with "nicest" as you shouldn't look like you just came from a long day at sea world or just finished painting a house. This can also negatively affect the perception of you and how you might fit in the team.

Salary

Once you've gone through the initial application, art test, phone screen, and most likely an onsite interview process and if the company is interested, you will likely receive a job offer. This is a very exciting moment; however, before accepting, it is important to be pragmatic about the offer and make sure it actually works for you.

Some things to consider before accepting the offer: cost of living can vary greatly depending on the location of the company. It's important to do some research into how much it actually costs to live in a location. This includes your rent, utilities, food, and any other bills like student loans or car payments. Be realistic with your math. You never want to be in a position where you're cutting corners on actual hard bills you need to pay by thinking "well I can make it work if I only eat Ramen every other day and skip lunch 3 times a week." While you can eat Ramen for lunch every other day, this sort of thinking can get you in trouble if you're just barely making it and some unexpected expense comes up down the road or worse, something happens to the company. It is okay to ask for more money upfront; this is called a counter offer.

Don't be afraid to counter offer. Keep in mind when preparing a counter offer, what's reasonable and realistic for the position and location. Eating only Ramen every day is one extreme while you shouldn't go too far in the other direction. Assuming you need a three bedroom house for just yourself as well as brand new car may be a little too far in the other direction of expectations. So temper your counter offer accordingly. It's important to remember that if a company is making you an offer they're interested in you and won't walk away if you ask for a little more money. Some companies' offers are solid and they won't budge on the initial offer while others have room for negotiation built in. It really doesn't hurt to ask especially if it's the difference between you being able to live on the salary or not. Additionally, it's a better idea to ask up front for more as opposed to asking for a raise after being there for 3 months once you realize the salary isn't enough.

Be Prepared to Get the Job

This may seem like a funny thing to say; however, there is a possibility if you apply to a company you may get a job offer. This should be great news; however, time and time again people starting out don't always consider what that actually means. First, unless you live in a major hotspot for games—California, Seattle, or Austin—you will have to move. Maybe this statement doesn't hit home. It could mean moving away from your family, significant other, and friends, possibly ending or breaking an apartment lease. Also, the best course of action is to have a serious discussion with your significant other prior to applying for work. If they're set on not moving or want to move to a location that doesn't have game-related work you should be prepared to face some hard life decisions.

Also the other thing to realize is there is a cost to moving, setting up utilities, and signing a new apartment or house lease. Most game companies will provide some relocation assistance; however, that money often comes after the move. If you don't have the money on hand it's often a good idea to look into borrowing money from family, the bank, or getting a credit card.

Conclusion

Oftentimes when preparing a portfolio, it's hard to see beyond the initial goal of finishing the portfolio. Even seeing slightly beyond that goal and actually applying, it's hard to know the ins and outs that happen. Hopefully this chapter has been helpful at shining a light on some of the behind-the-scenes and superfluous aspects of applying for a game job.

Index

C

Capturing of motion data, *see* Motion capture (Mo-cap)
CDs, *see* Creative directors (CDs)
CG, *see* Computer graphics (CG)
Character
    in concept art design, 142–144
    effects, 192–194
    interactions in animation design, 119–120
    pipelines, 131
    rig from Super Fuse Ball, 69
Character artists, 13, 29, 123–124; *see also* Concept artists
    adaptability, 131
    advice for new people in game industry, 39
    anatomy, 31–33
    "attention to detail" exercise, 127–128
    clothing, 33–35
    color, 33–35
    history, 126–127
    key items, 124
    key skills, 30, 129
    misconceptions, 39–40
    mistakes, 129
    personality, 130–131
    physically based materials, 37–38
    process, 38–39
    software programs, 35–36
    stylization, 124–126
    textures, 36–37
    user-generated content, 132
    weapons, 127, 128
Character art portfolio, *see* Character artists
Clothing in character design, 33–35
Collaboration, 10–11
Collision creation, 172
Color in character design, 33–35
Combo map in VFX art design, 96
Communication
    in concept art, 46
    in technical art design, 72–73
    in VFX art design, 97
Complacency, 204
Computer graphics (CG), 124

Concept artists, 13, 41, 44–45, 133–134; *see also* Character artists; Environment artists; Technical artists (TA); User Interface artists (UI artists); Visual effect artists (VFX artists)
    advice for new people in game industry, 49–50, 146
    alien weapon exploration by Tim McBurnie, 44
    anatomy, 136–138
    "attention to detail" exercise, 138–142
    average day, 49
    characters, 142–144
    communication, 46
    context, 45–46
    environments, 138, 139
    exploration, 43–44
    invention, 135–136
    key skills, 41–43
    misconceptions, 50
    mistakes, 134
    robot companions for sci-fi game, 136
    solid, 134
    style, 134–135
    subject matter, 135
    thumbnails, 47–49
    visual story telling, 46–47
    weapons, 144–145
Concept art portfolio; *see also* Concept artists
Conceptualization, 83–85
Content in environmental design, 149
Core animations, 118–119
Counter offer, 211
Cover letters, 197–199
Creative directors (CDs), 49
Creativity, 14
Criticism, 106–107
Crowfather from *Darksiders II*, 34
Cultural fit, 210
Cycles in animation design, 116–117

D

Darksiders
    Straga from, 130
    war from, 118